The FLIGHT of BONNIE PRINCE CHARLIE

Bonnie Prince Charlie on horseback in bronze by Anthony Stones, the only statue of the Prince in the British Isles. It stands in Derby where his march south ended before he retreated back to Scotland on 'Black Friday', 5 December 1745.

The FLIGHT of
BONNIE PRINCE
CHARLIE

HUGH DOUGLAS & MICHAEL J. STEAD

SUTTON PUBLISHING

First published in 2000 by
Sutton Publishing Limited · Phoenix Mill
Thrupp · Stroud · Gloucestershire · GL5 2BU

British Library Cataloguing in Publication Data
A catalogue record for this book is available from the British Library.

ISBN 0 7509 1989 2

Endpapers: front, mighty Blaven dominates the south Skye landscape; *back*, Glen Shiel, where Prince Charlie hid a whole day on the open hillside.

Typeset in 11/14.5 pt Bembo.
Typesetting and origination by
Sutton Publishing Limited.
Printed in Great Britain by
The Bath Press, Bath.

CONTENTS

The Prince had to cross many treacherous fast-running rivers like this one in Glen Moriston during his flight.

PREFACE

The flight of Bonnie Prince Charlie was one of history's great manhunts. It created Scotland's most treasured legend during five rain-soaked months of a Highland summer of 1746, when Charles Edward, heir to the Stuart dynasty, was hunted down ruthlessly after defeat at Culloden brought his '45 Jacobite rising to a bloody end. It tells of great courage and endurance, of bravery, and the loyalty of Highland followers who guarded him faithfully, rejecting the £30,000 reward King George II offered for his capture. They spirited him from mainland hide-outs to the far Hebridean isles and back again, fed him, clothed him and hid him in their homes and in caves located in the mountains. Finally they brought him back to Loch nan Uamh, where the 'rash adventure' of the Forty-Five rising had begun, to escape to France.

The Flight of Bonnie Prince Charlie is set against the ever-changing dramatic landscapes and wild seascapes of the West Highlands and Hebrides, and the story of it is told in pictures and in the words and thoughts of those who participated in it. Memoirs of the Prince's closest confidants, such as John William O'Sullivan, Lord Elcho, Lord George Murray and John Murray of Broughton, give the background to the adventure while the narrative is brought to life through vivid accounts of ordinary followers, collected by the Reverend Robert Forbes, Episcopalian Bishop of Ross and Caithness, in the years following Prince Charlie's escape. These were published more than a century later under the title *The Lyon in Mourning*. As well as the charismatic prince himself, Flora MacDonald, Neil MacEachain, Skye boatman Donald MacLeod and the people of the Scottish Highlands are the heroes and heroines of Prince Charlie's months 'on the wing'.

While the words are largely those of Prince Charlie's followers, guardians and friends, the book does not set out to eulogise a flawed man, but to show how a legend was created out of hardship and adversity.

Prince Charles Edward, *c.* 1750; after Hussey.

ACKNOWLEDGEMENTS

We are grateful to all who helped us during our journey in the steps of Bonnie Prince Charlie after Culloden: from the battlefield to Borrodale, to the Long Island of the Outer Hebrides, over the sea and across Skye from Uig to Elgol, then through many West Highland glens where Prince Charlie found shelter. We received generous help all the way, and thank particularly the staff of the National Trust for Scotland's centres at Culloden and Glenfinnan, Fiona Marwick of the West Highland Museum, Fort William, and Maggie MacDonald, Librarian at the Museum of the Isles at Armadale, Skye. The lovely little museum at Kildonan on South Uist, close to Flora MacDonald's birthplace, was a most welcome discovery. The present owners of Gorthlick, Invergarry, Borrodale, Monkstadt and Nunton, houses associated with the Prince's flight, kindly supplied information and permitted us to photograph the buildings and their surroundings. The libraries of Skye, Inverness, Fort Augustus and Stornoway willingly answered questions and provided information and advice. To all of them, and to Clive Burton, Amelia Gregor and Keeta Campbell, who have contributed their expert knowledge, we are grateful.

Finally, we extend our thanks to all those people of the West Highlands and Hebrides who welcomed us so generously into their homes and lives. Wherever we went we met with courtesy, helpfulness and kindness worthy of the hospitality their forebears offered the Prince while they were sheltering him. Our summer among them was very similar to that which the Prince experienced in 1746 – gales, rain storms, sunshine, showers and days that began soaking wet and ended in those glorious sunsets which make the Highlands of Scotland unforgettable. We have tried to record the Prince's journey in all these moods.

Hugh Douglas
Michael J. Stead

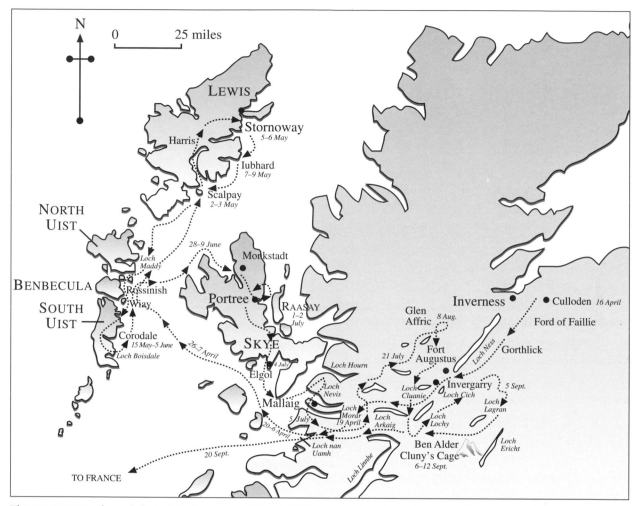

The great escape from defeat at Culloden on 16 April 1746 to departure from Loch nan Uamh on 19/20 September.

CREDITS FOR ADDITIONAL ILLUSTRATIONS

We are grateful to the following people and organisations for supplying images for use in the book:

p. 92 (top, left), Ashmolean Museum, Oxford; p. 151 (top, left), Bibliothèque nationale de France; p. 144, from W.B. Blaikie's *Itinerary of Prince Charles Edward Stuart*; p. 93 (bottom, left), from James Boswell's *Journal of a Tour to the Hebrides with Samuel Johnson*, 1852 edition; p. 103, John Campbell; p. 149, Clan Cameron Museum, Achnacarry, Spean Bridge; p. 58, Hugh Douglas; p. 62, from John S. Gibson's *Ships of the Forty-Five*; pp. 26, 27, National Galleries of Scotland; p. viii, Donald Nicholas Collection; p. 4, The Royal Collection © 2000, Her Majesty Queen Elizabeth II; pp. 56 (top, left), 100, West Highland Museum, Fort William.

BONNIE PRINCE CHARLIE – THE RASH ADVENTURER

The people of London danced in the streets, marvelled at fantastic firework shows and enjoyed the free bread and wine handed out for three nights running. They were celebrating the birth of a son and heir to their King, James VII of Scotland and II of England, on 10 June 1688. In Scotland, there was little to celebrate. Neither Lowland Presbyterians nor Episcopalians had any love for the King who had once lived among them, or his open practice of Roman Catholicism. Significantly, the celebrations were more joyous in Rome, where a three-day holiday was declared, oxen were roasted and fountains flowed with wine. The reason for Rome's jubilation was simple: the new Prince, James Francis Edward, would be baptised in the Roman Catholic faith, bringing about the restoration of a Catholic monarchy to England after a century and a half.

Within six months everything had changed: gossip persisted that the baby was not the King's child, but a changeling smuggled into the royal palace in a warming pan – this was believable since Queen Mary Beatrice had already given birth to five children, all of whom had died in infancy. More important than such scurrilous scandal was an invitation to the King's Protestant son-in-law, William of Orange, to bring an army to England, and James' flight with his wife and infant son into exile in France. They called this the Glorious Revolution, but it was also the genesis of Jacobitism.

The 'warming pan' baby can hardly be blamed for ensuring that when he grew up his own son entered the world in a manner that left no room for doubt. James married the Polish Princess Clementina Sobieska and her first accouchement at the Muti Palace in Rome was as public an event as one of the King's own levees: on the last day of 1720, when Clementina was delivered of a fine, strong, healthy boy, cardinals representing the three nations of England, Scotland and Ireland were present, alongside others from the Holy See and Spain and France. James himself knelt at a prie-dieu nearby and in the background the nobility of the Court watched.

The moment the baby had been swaddled in consecrated garments he was placed beneath a richly embroidered canopy to hold his first levee. The most scintillating leaders of Rome's brilliant society paid homage, cardinals blessed him and nobles who had chosen to follow the Stuarts into exile pressed the child's tiny hand to their lips and felt a fresh surge of loyalty coursing through their veins. Immediately afterwards the Bishop of Montefiascone, who had married James and Clementina not a year before, baptised the Prince in the little Chapel of La Madonna dell'Archetto behind the palace.

He was given the names Charles after his great-grandfather, Charles I, who was beheaded in 1649, Edward after England's only royal saint, Louis after the King of France, Philip after the King of Spain, Casimir after the kings of Poland and Sylvester because he was born on St Sylvester's Day. Oddly, in view of the Stuarts' strong associations with Scotland and Ireland, Andrew and Patrick were not included. The baby was immediately created Prince of Wales, and within the family circle was addressed as Charles. His father's affectionate name for him was the Italian Carluccio, while his mother used the Polish Carlusu and the French referred to him as Edouard. He was almost never called Charles Edward, and the name Prince Charlie, which was to follow later, was a rendering of the Gaelic 'Tearlach' into English. But by then Prince Charlie was the legendary Bonnie Prince.

In spite of all the appearance of a British monarch presenting his heir to his people when Charles Stuart was born in 1720, the Stuarts had been separated from their throne for more than a quarter of a century. The new Prince's grandfather, James VII and II, had died in exile in 1701. His father now 'ruled' as King James VIII and III, and was known as the 'King over the Water' to his friends and the Pretender to his enemies.

In both England and Scotland much had changed over these years. The two countries were welded into one kingdom under a single parliament in 1707, and at the death of Queen Anne in 1714, the Crown passed to the Elector of Hanover, His Majesty King George I to his friends and 'German Geordie' to those who would have been glad to send him back to Hanover.

James and his father had tried with the help of King Louis XV of France to mount restoration attempts in the 1690s, 1708 and 1715, and with Spanish support in 1719, but failed every time. On his return from the 1719 invasion James married Clementina Sobieska, and Charles Edward was born at the end of 1720. A second son, Henry, followed five years later, and was given the title Duke of York. Unfortunately, by this time Clementina had become difficult, and then mentally unstable; eventually she abandoned her family to live in a convent. James worked manfully to be a good father and prepare his sons for their future role, especially to groom Charles for kingship. He instilled in the young Prince the passionate belief in his divine right to reign and a sure conviction that

God would lead them back to their lost inheritance. The Jacobite world who flocked to Rome to pay homage served to reinforce these beliefs, and from his earliest days Charles prepared for the day he would lead his loyal subjects against the usurping Hanoverians.

At the age of fourteen Charles was allowed a brief glimpse of war when he joined the Spanish Army besieging Gaeta in southern Italy. On his return to Rome he worked hard to prepare himself for the rigours of campaigning to oust King George. He hardened his body with long walks and hunting expeditions in the Albano hills around Rome, often hunting all day then returning to play his cello long into the night, on occasion refusing to go to bed at all. He simply threw a greatcoat over himself and dozed until it was time to set out again. His servants were often worn out, but Charles knew no tiredness. His brother came from a very different mould: he grew up to be a deeply religious, sensitive, introspective young man unable to share his sibling's interests.

Throughout Charles' childhood the Pretender was unable to find any support for another rising, but at last the political climate warmed for him with the outbreak of the War of Austrian Succession in the early 1740s. Although war had not been declared against Britain, Louis XV decided to invade England, using the Stuarts to justify his attack. He laid his plan deviously: the Pretender in Rome would be asked to furnish all the proclamations he needed, but neither the Pretender nor his son would take part – only when London was in French hands would a Stuart be brought over. James was cautious, but when news of the scheme (but not of Louis' duplicity) reached the young Prince's ears his impetuosity could not be contained.

Charles persuaded his father to issue an immediate declaration of regency in his favour and to permit him to travel to France in such secrecy that neither spies, King Louis, nor Charles' own servants heard a whisper of his plan – not even his own brother knew of it. On 8 January 1744 he announced that the Duke of Caserta had invited him to join a hunting expedition, and sent his staff ahead to prepare for his arrival. That night the Prince dined with his brother Henry, but pretended he was weary and retired to bed early. He then slipped off to his father's room by a secret passage, said his farewells and left: the two were never to meet again.

By an elaborate subterfuge Charles left by the southern gate of the city, rode secretly round the walls and by daylight was on his way north. To throw spies and his brother off the scent a story was spread that he had been injured in a fall from his horse and would be delayed. Accompanied by his groom, Charles rode hard over treacherous icy roads to reach Genoa, some 300 miles away, in just five days. The only problem – and he was not aware of it at the time – was that he was recognised as he passed through Florence, and by 21 January word of the Stuart Prince's strange, furtive journey was on its way to London via the British envoy and spymaster in the city, Sir Horace Mann.

Prince Charlie at Holyroodhouse in 1745 by John Pettie.

Charles planned to sail to a port on the French Mediterranean coast and ride up the Rhône valley to Paris, but storms delayed him long enough for Mann to alert Admiral Thomas Matthews, commander of a Royal Navy fleet then in the Mediterranean. Matthews missed Charles by a whisker as he entered Antibes harbour, but now the Prince encountered another difficulty — the French authorities would not allow him to land because plague had closed most northern Mediterranean ports. Charles set to with all his guile and powers of persuasion: first he got rid of Matthews by sending the Navy on a wild goose chase after an empty ship in which they thought he was hidden, then he prevailed on the governor to break the quarantine cordon and permit him to leave for Paris on 29 January. Ten days later he was in the French capital, in his own words, 'rendu but triumphant'.

King Louis was appalled to find the unwanted Stuart Prince on his doorstep and feared his presence might betray the invasion plan, especially as the people of Paris were giving a noisy hero's welcome to this charismatic young man who had come to lead their fight against the old enemy across the Channel. What the French King did not know was that the secret was already out, betrayed by François de Bussy, his own envoy in London.

Charles moved to the Channel coast to sail with the invaders, but there he found nothing but confusion. Moreover, the Royal Navy was waiting like a cat at a mouse hole to pounce as the French left port. The British had no need to attack, however — their job was done for them by a storm, which caused such severe damage that the invasion had to be called off. Louis then declared war officially, and embarked on a new campaign against the British in Flanders, using Charles' untimely arrival as a convenient excuse for his own failure.

Beside himself with fury, the Prince told Lord Sempill, one of his father's agents in Paris, that if King Louis would help him no further he would hire a fishing boat and sail to Scotland where he felt sure his faithful Highlanders would rally to him. And that was virtually what he did. In the frigate *Duteillay*, hired from the French Navy by a wealthy Franco-Irish merchant and privateer, Antoine Walsh, and accompanied by a larger warship, the *Elisabeth*, he sailed for Scotland on 12 July 1745. By sheer bad luck the *Elisabeth* was attacked and badly damaged by a British warship and forced to turn back, so Charles arrived in Scotland with only one ship, few arms and seven close companions, who became known in subsequent accounts as the Seven Men of Moidart.

On 22 July he made landfall in Scotland at Barra Head, the southernmost tip of the Outer Hebrides, the myriad of bare islands that stretches for a hundred disordered miles off Scotland's north-west coast. The Outer Hebrides run from the broad island that begins as Lewis and ends as Harris, through North Uist, Benbecula and South Uist to a tail of magically named small islands — Eriskay, Barra, Vatersay, Sandray, Pabbay, Mingulay and Berneray — to Barra Head. With so many small islands separated by sounds and narrow straits these islands are aptly known as the Long Island as if they were a single landmass.

At Barra one of the party, who knew the island well, went ashore in search of a pilot to guide them among the islands. Callum MacNeil, none other than the piper to the MacNeil chief of Barra, was brought on board to show a safe way northwards to Eriskay, where they had decided to land. Although Charles Stuart had never experienced such bitter rain as beat against him while the *Duteillay* nosed through the Sound of Barra in search of a landing place on Eriskay, he did not complain – his hunting expeditions in Italy had prepared him well for this moment. Since Eriskay had no harbour the Barra piper chose a small sandy beach set between two rocky promontories, but instead of a ceremonial stepping ashore such as the heir to the Stuart dynasty might have expected, his landing turned to farce. While one of the clansmen was carrying the Prince ashore on his shoulders a ship, possibly a British warship, appeared in the distance and everyone had to make a mad scramble to find a hiding place. Fortunately, the vessel did not see them, but for his safety it was decided that the Prince should remain on Eriskay that night.

Borrodale House, standing close to Loch nan Uamh, is the house most closely associated with Prince Charles. Here he rallied the clan chiefs on his arrival in 1745, and here he planned his escape to France after Culloden. The Royal Navy, hunting for the Prince, burned Borrodale down shortly after his second visit, but it was rebuilt much as it had been when he stayed there.

Glenfinnan. This monument, erected at the head of Loch Shiel in 1815, commemorates the raising of the Stuart standard on 19 August 1745. It is now in the care of the National Trust for Scotland.

Overleaf: At Glenfinnan, where the standard was raised, Loch Shiel is hemmed in by dark forbidding hills.

The spot where the Prince landed is now called Coilleag a' Phrionnsa, the Prince's Shore, and here a pink convolvulus grows, the only place in the Hebrides where the flower is to be found. Tradition has it that the plant, *Calystegia Soldanella*, a sea bindweed known as Fluir-a-Phrionnsa (the Prince's Flower) in Gaelic, grew from seeds that fell from his pocket as he landed.

Eriskay belonged to the Clanranald branch of Clan Donald, the members of which were good Catholics and loyal friends to the Cause, so word was sent to the nearest of their chiefs, Clanranald's half-brother Alexander MacDonald of Boisdale, on the neighbouring island of South Uist. Boisdale was appalled to learn that the Prince had arrived without French support and rushed to Eriskay to tell Charles that the clans were not ready to rise, so he should go home. 'I am come home, Sir,' replied Charles, 'and will entertain no notion at all of returning to that place from whence I came; for that I am persuaded my faithful Highlanders will stand by me.'

The following day, 25 July, the *Duteillay* sailed to the mainland and Prince Charles landed at Loch nan Uamh, a remote sea loch opening on to the Sound of Arisaig, some 30 miles west of Fort William. The loch was a perfect place, lying on a track between Lochailort and Arisaig, and difficult for government detachments to reach. This, too, was staunchly Catholic country, belonging to loyal clans, with a mountainous hinterland where the Prince could be concealed should enemies come in search of him. The name Loch nan Uamh means loch of the caves, an apt name, for around it there are many caves and crevices and it was in some of these that Prince Charlie would take refuge during his flight after Culloden.

At Borrodale House on the shore of the loch Charles spent a fortnight meeting clan chiefs to persuade them to call out their clansmen to fight, and writing letters and sending messengers to win waverers over. The response of the clansmen was disappointing: a few willingly supported the Prince, but many hesitated or took their lead from the two great Skye chiefs, Sir Alexander MacDonald of Sleat or Norman MacLeod of MacLeod and flatly refused to 'come out' for the Cause. It was not loyalty to King George that kept Sleat and MacLeod out of the '45 rising, but fear that the time was not ripe. Sleat had made it clear the moment Charles landed that he would not support a campaign without French backing, while MacLeod simply went back on his word after originally agreeing to follow the Prince. Both chiefs also held back out of fear of losing their estates as had happened to so many chiefs after the rising of 1715, and because the government threatened that unless they supported it they might face prosecution over a scandal involving the kidnapping and deportation of their clansmen to the American colonies as bonded servants. The Lord President in Edinburgh, Duncan Forbes of Culloden, used this last threat effectively to persuade Sleat and MacLeod to throw in their lot with Hanover and to raise militia regiments to help the Duke of

Cumberland's redcoats. However, many of their clansmen marched with the Jacobites – and the Prince even wore Sleat's shirts while in hiding.

In spite of this disappointing response, Prince Charlie remained determined to fight, and as proof of his serious intent, sent the *Duteilley* back to France. Now there could be no going home. On 11 August he moved south to Kinlochmoidart, where he was joined by John Murray of Broughton, whom he had known in Rome and whom he now appointed his Secretary. The Jacobites were scoring minor successes in the Highlands already: Captain John Sweetenham of Guise's Regiment was taken near the head of the Corrieyairack Pass on his way to Fort William, and at High Bridge on the River Spean a handful of Highlanders and a piper led by MacDonald of Tiendrish and MacDonald of Keppoch captured two companies of Royal Scots marching from Perth to reinforce Fort William.

Glenfinnan, at the head of Loch Shiel, midway between Arisaig and Fort William, was chosen as the rallying point where the Stuart standard was to be raised, and on 19 August Charles sailed up Loch Shiel, uncertain whether he would have an army to lead at the end of the day. Many clan chiefs still felt unsure and unprepared, and continued to hold back so that when he landed at Glenfinnan he had only 50 Clanranald men guarding him, 150 Morar MacDonalds, a similar number of Gordons led by Glenbucket

Overleaf: The Sound of Barra separates South Uist from Eriskay, the island on which Prince Charles Edward Stuart first set foot in Scotland.

Glenfinnan statue. The man in Highland dress surmounting the monument was intended to be Prince Charlie. Unfortunately, the sculptor, John Greenshields, was shown the wrong portrait and consequently modelled his statue on George Lockhart of Carnwath, one of the Prince's followers.

and a few MacGregors under James Mohr MacGregor, son of that notorious Scottish Robin Hood, Rob Roy MacGregor. He did not know it, but James Mohr was as treacherous as his father and was present at Glenfinnan in a dual capacity – to bring followers to the Prince and to report everything he saw back to the government.

It was three in the afternoon before the sound of bagpipes heralded the arrival of 700 of Cameron of Lochiel's men and 300 Keppoch

THE STEWART SUCCESSION

THE STEWARTS

Robert II 1371–90
Son of Robert Bruce's daughter
Marjorie and Walter, High Steward
of Scotland

Robert III 1390–1406
John of Carrick, took title Robert III
because the name John was considered
unlucky

James I 1406–37
A prisoner in England for eighteen
years, murdered at Perth by Sir Robert
Graham

James II 1437–60
Crowned at age of six. Known as 'fiery
face' because of a birthmark. Killed by a
bursing cannon at Roxburgh Castle

James III 1460–88
Succeeded at age of nine. Struggle
against rebellious nobles led to civil war
and defeat at Sauchieburn, where he
was murdered as he fled the battlefield

James IV 1488–1513
Crowned at age of fifteen. His reign saw
the arts flourish in Scotland, but he went
to war with England in 1512 and was
killed at Flodden in 1513

James V 1513–42
An infant when he succeeded. Auld
Alliance with France led to war with
England. Scots Army defeated at Solway
Moss and he died of a broken heart
three weeks later

Mary Queen of Scots 1542–67
Only a few days old when she became Queen.
Educated in France and married Dauphin, who
died. She was implicated in the murder of her
second husband, Lord Darnley. Married Earl of
Bothwell and was forced to abdicate in 1567.
Prisoner in England until she was implicated in a
plot to assassinate Queen Elizabeth and was tried
and executed at Fotheringhay Castle,
Northamptonshire, in 1587. Mary adopted the
spelling 'Stuart' because the French language does
not incorporate the letter 'W'.

THE STUARTS

James VI 1567–1625
Mary's son by Lord Darnley. Born in 1566 and succeeded the following year. James succeeded to throne of England as James I on death of Queen Elizabeth in 1603

Charles I 1625–48
Quarrelled with English and Scottish subjects – with House of Commons in England and Presbyterian Church in Scotland. This led to Civil War, when Charles was arrested and tried and executed in 1649

Charles II 1660–85
Proclaimed King of Scots on father's death, but Scottish efforts to restore him in England resulted in defeat at Worcester. Remained in exile in France and Holland until 1660. He then made enemies of the Scots by trying to impose episcopacy on the country

James VII and II 1685–8
Opposition to his open profession of Roman Catholicism, and birth of a son who would be brought up a Catholic, led to the Glorious Revolution, when James fled to France

William of Orange 1688–1702 and Mary 1688–94
Reigned jointly until Mary's death in 1694. William defeated first Jacobite attempts to win back crowns of England and Scotland. William died in 1702

Anne 1702–14
During Anne's reign Scotland and England were united under one Parliament (1707), and Protestant succession was secured through the Electors of Hanover, descendants of James VI's daughter Elizabeth

1714 Elector George of Hanover succeeded as George I

THE JACOBITES
In exile James VII and II failed in attempts to regain Scotland, England and Ireland. He died in France in exile in 1701.

James VIII and III
The Old Pretender (1701–66). Attempted risings in 1708, 1715 and 1719

Charles III
The Young Pretender (1766–88)

Henry IX
Cardinal Duke of York (1788–1807)

Loch Shiel. No road ran alongside the loch in 1745, so the Prince had to be rowed 17 miles up the loch to Glenfinnan where his standard was raised on 19 August 1745.

The commemorative cairn at High Bridge, near Spean Bridge. The first blood of the '45 campaign was drawn here before the standard was raised at Glenfinnan. At the narrow bridge across the River Spean a small party of MacDonalds and a piper ambushed two companies of Royal Scots on their way to reinforce the garrison at Fort William. After a running fight the government force surrendered, and was marched to Glenfinnan to watch Prince Charlie's standard being raised.

MacDonalds. This small army, the Royal Scots prisoners and Captain Sweetenham watched the elderly Jacobite Duke of Atholl raise the standard and the Roman Catholic Bishop Hugh MacDonald bless it. Prince Charles, Tearlach to his Gaelic-speaking followers, made 'a short but very Pathetick speech' and was cheered to the echo, Murray of Broughton recounted, although many of the Highlanders probably spoke no English and had no idea what he was saying.

In the meantime, King George's General Sir John Cope was marching north unaware of all that was happening in Morar and Moidart until he met Captain Sweetenham at Dalnacardoch, north of Blair Atholl. The Captain had been released on parole, which he immediately broke by going straight to Cope to report that the Prince was planning to ambush him with 3,000 men at the Corrieyairack Pass, one of the wildest and most remote places through which Cope had to pass on the road north. The General decided to play safe and marched to Inverness instead.

This left the road to Edinburgh clear, and within days Charles swept south, avoiding Stirling Castle, which had a strong garrison, to capture the Scottish capital and proclaim his father King. Before the end of September he had routed Cope's Army at Prestonpans and the Stuarts were restored to Scotland. For six glorious weeks Charles reigned as Prince Regent at the Palace of Holyroodhouse, holding court each day or riding out to

Duddingston to review his Army, adored by all who had dreamed of a Stuart restoration, and many who were simply mesmerised by his success. After Prestonpans his Highlanders believed he – and they – were invincible and already the legend of Bonnie Prince Charlie was taking shape.

Alongside this success, however, there were hard decisions to be made, and these sowed the seeds of future troubles. He formed a Council of War, in which his Scottish and Irish leaders disagreed, and he argued with his Lieutenant-General Lord George Murray. It took six weeks for Charles and his Council to make the decision to invade England, and even then they argued over which route to follow – east by Newcastle or west by Carlisle. At last, on 14 November, the Jacobite Army marched south by the western route, captured Carlisle Castle and was soon in Lancashire, looking for the English recruits they expected to find waiting for them. Apart from Manchester, where a regiment was gathered, few joined them.

The Battle of Prestonpans monument commemorating the Jacobite victory, which convinced Prince Charles that his Highlanders were invincible.

It was clear that neither professed Jacobite leaders nor the common people in England were prepared to fight for the Prince, so at Derby the leaders – even the Irish who usually sided with him – forced Charles to agree to return to Scotland to await reinforcements from France. Without losing a battle Prince Charlie was in retreat. Overnight his character changed: he became a sullen, morose, uncharismatic man who trailed behind his men all the way back to Carlisle and into Scotland. By the end of December he was in Glasgow, where he was made far from welcome. Charles still had not been defeated, and he won another victory at Falkirk in January 1746, yet he decided to retreat northwards into the Highlands. As he did so his Army scored several smaller successes, including the capture of Inverness and Fort Augustus, the Hanoverian fort midway down the Great Glen. Only Fort William held out against him.

The Prince himself narrowly escaped capture in mid-February, while staying at Moy Hall, home of 'Colonel Anne' Mackintosh, who had raised men for the Prince while her husband was away serving with the government Army. The Earl of Loudoun, Hanoverian commander at Inverness, set a trap but Charles was warned and managed to escape, dressed in his night attire, and hide in nearby woods. There were only two casualties of the incident, Donald MacCrimmon, the MacLeod piper, who was shot dead, and the Prince himself: Charles caught a severe chill, which turned to a fever, probably scarlet fever, and put him out of action for the best part of March.

In the meantime, the Hanoverians were closing in. King George's son William, Duke of Cumberland had been recalled from Flanders when the Jacobites invaded England, and as Commander-in-Chief of government forces in Britain he trailed the rebels north to Scotland. He left it to the crusty old Lieutenant-General Henry Hawley, commander in Scotland, to deal with the rebels north of the border, and Hawley's first encounter with the rebels on the battlefield at Falkirk was not a happy one. Neither he nor his officers distinguished themselves, and, while he may not have been soundly beaten, he suffered the indignity of watching his men flee before the Highlanders' broadswords. Hawley's temper was not improved by having to admit to Cumberland 'such a scandalous cowardice I never saw before'. However, he managed to pass the blame on to his officers, and had half a dozen of them court martialled.

Cumberland himself now went north to take charge, and as soon as he set foot in Scotland on 30 January he began to scourge the country with fire and cruelty, a taste of what was to follow Culloden. Since the Prince had retreated into the mountainous Highlands, Cumberland and Hawley moved their men to Aberdeen where they settled down comfortably to prepare for the final showdown with the rebels.

Only the counties of Banff, Moray and Nairn separated the two armies, and both knew that the battle must follow soon.

Edinburgh Castle. Like Stirling, Edinburgh Castle refused to surrender when Charles arrived at the city gates on 16 September. The following day his Highlanders burst into the city when the gates were opened to allow a coach to leave, and the Scottish capital was his – all except the castle, which never surrendered.

Stirling Castle. Charles never captured this castle, which had a long association with Scottish freedom and was a favourite home of his Stewart ancestors. The castle held out, but the Prince boldly marched past it and on to Edinburgh. The following year he besieged Stirling briefly, but failed to take it.

The Palace of Holyroodhouse, Edinburgh, had been a royal residence for centuries, and was rebuilt and extended by the Prince's grandfather, James VII and II (while Duke of York), who commissioned portraits of eighty-nine Scottish monarchs for its great gallery. Charles held court here for six glorious weeks.

THE END OF A BAD AFFAIR

Charles Edward Stuart recovered slowly from the fever he had contracted after his narrow escape at Moy, and was comfortably settled in Inverness during the first days of April. Here he was among friends and lived well as the accounts of James Gib, Master of his Household, testify. On Friday 11 April Gib bought a cow, a pair of lambs, poultry and eggs, one-and-sixpence-worth of fresh cod as well as pepper and cloves to season it all. The following day oysters and a hare were added to the royal table.

The Prince's men were faring less well. Money had run so low he had to pay his troops in meal, and when that ran out he ordered Robert Strange, engraver, to prepare copper plates to print paper money. These were ready only a few days before Culloden and were never used. They were found in a bog close to the battlefield more than

Inverness Castle. Although there had been a fortress there for many centuries, the castle of Inverness dates only from the nineteenth century, when it was rebuilt after Prince Charlie destroyed it in 1746 to prevent it from falling into enemy hands. The castle, which had a long and stormy history, was held by the Jacobites during both the 1715 and 1745 risings.

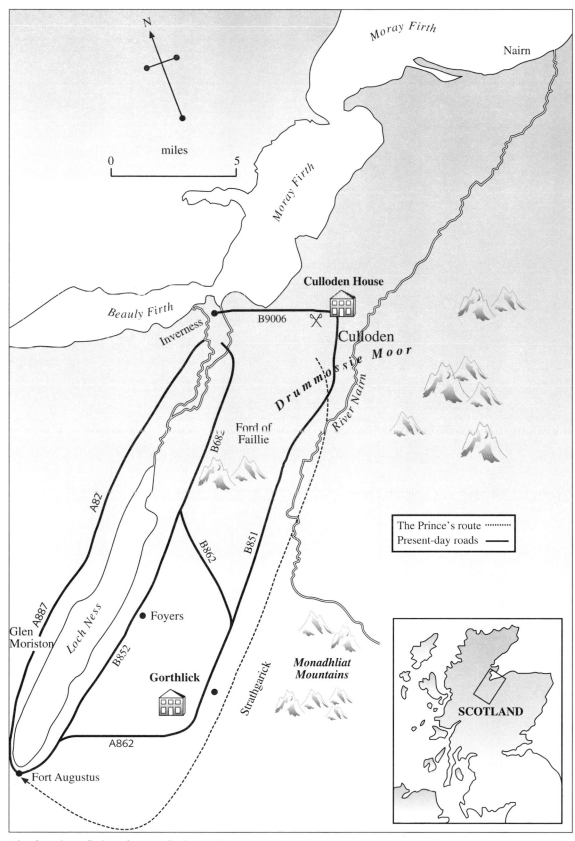

The first day's flight – from Culloden to Fort Augustus.

a hundred years later. Towards the end of March hopes rose when a French ship, the *Prince Charles*, arrived with money and supplies, but she was waylaid by the Royal Navy in the Pentland Firth and forced aground on the far northern coast of Caithness as she manoeuvred desperately to escape. Close on 200 men and more than £12,000 in cash were captured, and the leaders of a party sent north to recover the treasure were taken too.

The Prince by now appeared to have lost interest in the campaign and left much of the organisation to his closest leaders, which meant to his Irish favourites since he no longer trusted the Scots, who gave blunt and often unpalatable answers to every question he asked. In his account of the rising David Wemyss, Lord Elcho, wrote, 'Their [*sic*] was great discontent in his Army at this time both amongst the Officers and Soldiers . . . He paid his troops mostly in meal, which they did not like and very often mutiny'd, refused to obey orders, and Sometimes threw down their arms and went home.' Secretary John Murray of Broughton, who might have retrieved the situation, went down with the fever from which the Prince had just recovered, and his duties had to be handed over to John Hay of Restalrig, a man who was so utterly incompetent that the starving clansmen had to fend for themselves. For many this meant deserting to return to their clanlands.

The Prince was caught unprepared when news reached Inverness on Sunday 13 April that Cumberland had left Aberdeen on the 8th with a 9,000-strong army that was well trained, well equipped and well fed. On 12 April they reached the River Spey, where a Jacobite force under the Duke of Perth and Lord John Drummond, specially stationed there to oppose a crossing, retreated without firing a shot. To Cumberland's astonishment, the road to Inverness lay open. He camped at Alves the following day, the day Charles first learned of the enemy's departure from Aberdeen.

On the morning of 14 April Charles left Inverness and set up headquarters at Culloden House – by coincidence the home of Lord President Duncan Forbes, the man who had done more than any other Scot to hold many Highland clans loyal to the government. He was joined by Lochiel Camerons and Glen Garry Macdonnells as well as the Duke of Perth's men, who had to abandon their supplies of meal in their rush to get clear of Nairn just as the Hanoverians marched into the town at the opposite end.

Although he and Lord George Murray were barely on speaking terms by now, the Prince had the wisdom to send Murray to choose a battlefield that would suit the Highlanders, and with his experienced soldier's eye Murray proposed rough ground close to Dalcross Castle, which he knew could be defended easily. Charles could not accept a Scot's opinion without question, so he sent O'Sullivan to examine it. Of course the

The Battle of Culloden memorial cairn on Drummossie Moor, where the battle was fought, stands at a point midway between the positions the two armies held at the start of the engagement.

William Augustus, Duke of Cumberland, attributed to Joshua Reynolds.

Irishman returned with a better suggestion: Drummossie Moor, a stretch of uneven moorland a mile or so from Culloden House, high, open ground pitted with bogs and little lochans. From the depths of his military inexperience O'Sullivan pronounced that this place would offer protection to the Prince's left wing.

Lord George was aghast. 'Not one single souldier but would have been against such a ffeeld had their advice been askt,' he raged later. This was moorland that would allow Cumberland's men 'full use of their Cannon so as to anoy the Highlanders prodigiously before they could possibly make an attack'. There was no time to listen to arguments now, and Charles made his decision in O'Sullivan's favour – his Army would be drawn up on Drummossie Moor.

Positioning the clans caused further trouble. In the past Lord George had been accused of giving his Atholl men a safe position in the line of battle, so this time he assigned them to the right wing where they would be more exposed. This infuriated the MacDonalds who considered the right wing to be theirs by tradition, but Charles for once supported his Lieutenant-General and left the Clan Donald men sulking. As the arguments raged about the choice of field and clan positions, the weary, starving men were dismissed to rest or forage for food wherever they could.

Tuesday, 15 April was a miserable wild day with a strong north-north-east wind gusting sleety rain down the Moray Firth towards Inverness, whipping across both drenched armies. The Jacobites waited, but no attack came – instead Cumberland remained in his camp with his men who were in high spirits as they were celebrating their commander's twenty-fifth birthday. Charles decided to ambush the carousing Army, and ordered a night march on Cumberland's camp. The attack failed, partly due to incompetence of the Jacobite leaders and partly because of the terrible weather and the difficulty of rounding up their hungry, weary soldiers. Towards dawn it was called off.

When they returned to Culloden at about six o'clock on the morning of Wednesday 16 April Drummossie Moor was shrouded in a dank mist. From the Prince in the comfort of Culloden House down to the lowest clansman squatting on the open moor, spirits were as frigid as the day. A great many clansmen set out towards Inverness in search of food, while the remainder lay down to sleep where they were, many so exhausted that Cumberland's guns failed to wake them and they were callously bayoneted where they lay.

Lord George, Lochiel, Keppoch and even King Louis' envoy the Marquis d'Eguilles all tried to persuade the Prince to withdraw and avoid battle that day, but he refused. In the end he lost his temper and shouted, 'God damn it, are my orders still disobeyed? Fight where you will, gentlemen, the day is not ours.' But the decision to fight was not his:

The Prince is seen fleeing Culloden field on horseback in this satirical anti-Jacobite drawing.

TANDEM TRIUMPHANS,
Translated by the Duke of Cumberland.
— With the Point of His Sword. —

1 The Duke,
2 Lᵈ Albemarle,
3 The Young Chevalier,
4 Sullivan,

6 Lᵈ Kilmarnock,
7 Lady Ogilvy,
8 Lady Murry,
9 Culloden House,

CULLODEN – THE END OF THE '45

At Culloden, near Inverness, on Wednesday 16 April 1746 the '45 rising came to an end. This was an ill-matched fight – Prince Charlie's men were disheartened and ill equipped, while the Duke of Cumberland marched at the head of 9,000 well-trained, well-fed men, all raring for the fight.

Charles made a number of tactical errors, but none worse than rejecting Lord George Murray's choice of an easily defended battlefield well suited to his Highlanders, in favour of the uneven, open moorland of Drummossie Moor, proposed by John William O'Sullivan, a man with no military knowledge whatever. The Jacobites were hungry and so exhausted after a failed night ambush on Cumberland's Army the previous night that when the time came for them to be drawn up for battle, the leaders could muster fewer than half as many men as their enemy. They could not even agree on their line of battle, and the MacDonalds sulked because they had not been given the position on the right of the line, which they claimed was theirs by tradition.

The Well of the Dead. At this spring clansmen were killed while trying to drink.

Sunset on the battlefield.

Culloden field where the Prince's ill-prepared Army positioned to the left faced Cumberland's well-organised battle lines.

The battle began at about one o'clock when the Prince's cannon – too few and 'ill-served and ill-pointed' – fired ineffectually towards the enemy. Cumberland replied with deadly accurate fire, and when the Highlanders were given the order to charge they were raked by muskets and cut down by a wall of bayonets. Culloden, the last set battle ever fought on British soil, was over in little more than half an hour. While Cumberland settled down to eat his midday meal on a stone on the battlefield known to this day as the Cumberland stone, his men earned him the nickname 'the Butcher' by murdering fleeing Jacobites and many innocent people they came upon as well. And the Prince and those clansmen who managed to escape took to the hills where they were hunted down like animals.

One of the rough stones that mark the graves of the clans.

Background: *The valley of the River Nairn into Stratherrick.*

Cumberland was determined not to lose the initiative, so he quickly brought his Army into position, his men wading up to the waist at times to drag cannon through muddy waterholes and bogs. By one o'clock, they stood face to face with the Jacobites, Cumberland's 9,000 well-disciplined soldiers facing a Jacobite Army only half that size because many of Prince Charlie's men were still asleep or away foraging for food. Those on the field were already tired and hungry, but were now colder than ever because O'Sullivan had positioned them facing into the freezing rain and sleet, which continued to blow across the moor. Part of the Army was also hemmed in by the walls of the Culloden estate, while Cumberland's men were well set out with their backs to the bad weather and raring for a fight.

There was no time to discuss new orders so those of the previous two days were allowed to stand, with only one change – the Prince's battle lines were set a little further back. Officers were racing in all directions to bring up cannon and place their men in battle order, but in all the confusion a couple of the guns had to be left behind at Culloden House because there were not enough horses to drag them up.

There was still time for Charles' principal officers and the clans to bicker, however. The MacDonalds were still annoyed at not being given their place on the right wing and refused to move forward into a position that would leave them badly protected. This prevented the whole front line from spreading out to give the men more space. The Prince's first line of battle was mainly Highland, but his second comprised largely Lowland regiments and Scottish and Irish units from the French Army, behind whom stood the few cavalry he possessed. The Prince sat on a grey gelding on Balvaid Hill where he could survey the whole field. As final positions were being taken up Elcho turned to Lord George and asked how he thought the day would go. 'We are putting an end to a bad affair,' the Lieutenant-General answered grimly.

Between one and two o'clock in the afternoon the guns in the centre of the Highlanders' line fired. The battle, the last to be fought on British soil, had begun. Cumberland returned fire with devastating accuracy and tore holes in the ranks of the Highlanders: then his men moved forward. The clansmen were desperate to attack, but Murray held them back until he had the Prince's permission to move. When that came the MacDonalds, still sulking over the slight, stood their ground, sullen and angry, refusing to move ahead of the other front-line regiments. Then the right and centre raced forward, threw down their muskets and sped towards the enemy, but the men in the centre veered towards the right, preventing soldiers stationed on the right from engaging. They were shot down by deadly accurate fire like deer driven across a moor for sport, and those who escaped Hanoverian musket balls were bayoneted as they tried to flee.

Before two o'clock it was all over: 1,200 of Prince Charlie's soldiers lay dead, surrounded by as many more wounded or dying, while the Duke had lost only 364 men. In disarray the Jacobite Army was fleeing in all directions pursued by redcoats, while the Prince still sat on his horse on Balvaid Hill, too mesmerised to move.

A number of tales were told afterwards about the Prince's behaviour during the battle: it was claimed that his horse was shot under him as he watched the battle, and although that was denied by those who were at his side, he did pause at Fort Augustus that night to have a musket ball removed from his horse's neck. He probably had a narrow escape. The Prince's Italian valet Michele Vezzosi said that in the confusion Charles' bonnet and wig flew off and the valet recovered the wig as it became caught up in the pommel of his saddle.

It is not true, however, that Elcho called the Prince 'a damned cowardly Italian', though at times young David Wemyss's thoughts probably ran along such lines. Charles Edward Stuart had many faults: he listened to his Irish favourites, rejected the advice of wiser men, made unreasonable demands on his followers and he commanded his Army badly, but he was never a coward. As the Highland line crumbled he rode furiously among the men, urging them to hold fast. 'Rally in the name of God,' he shouted. 'Pray, gentlemen, return. Pray, stand with me, your Prince, but a moment – otherwise you ruin me, your country and yourselves; and God forgive you.' The words may not be exact, since Vezzosi, who reported them, was not actually present at that moment, but one can believe what he added: 'The mouths of murdering cannon spoke a louder and more persuasive language than all his promises and entreaties could do, though uttered in the most moving terms.'

O'Sullivan tried to persuade the Prince to flee. 'You see all is going to pot, you can be of no great succour,' he shouted to Charles, and then turned to Adjutant-General Colonel Robert O'Shea: 'Before a general deroute which will soon be, seize upon the Prince and take him off.' Catching hold of the Prince's bridle, he ordered O'Shea to have Charles escorted from the field. Through tears Charles muttered, 'Do as you wish, only go now.' Lochiel's uncle 'Major Kennedy' then led him away.

It seems incredible that no thought had been given to how the Prince should escape in the event of defeat – perhaps those around him with influence shared his sense of invincibility. Certainly the Jacobite Army had won every battle it had fought during the '45 and the majority of the skirmishes as well, so it had reason to expect to win Culloden too – up to that last minute when it must have been obvious to all that it was a beaten force. The only piece of advice O'Shea was given came from that most unreliable of men, O'Sullivan. He ordered that if they were followed by Cumberland's dragoons he should stand and fight to allow the Prince time to escape – nothing more. And with that Prince Charlie set out on

Overleaf: After his defeat at Culloden Prince Charles Edward rode swiftly southward up the remote and increasingly desolate valley of the River Nairn into Stratherrick, accompanied only by a guide and a handful of followers. By late evening he had put the best part of 20 miles between himself and the battlefield.

the five-month long adventure that has become one of history's legendary escape stories.

The first imperative was to get the Prince as far away from Drummossie as possible. With only O'Shea and his men to guard him and accompanied by Hay of Restalrig, a few Scots officers, and faithful Thomas Sheridan, his old tutor who had followed him all the way from Rome, Charles rode southward across the moor towards Daviot into the valley of the River Nairn. Still mounted on the grey gelding he had ridden during the battle, he reached the Ford of Faillie where he encountered O'Sullivan and Elcho and stopped to discuss with them where he ought to go next. According to Elcho the Prince was 'in a deplorable state' and so obsessed with the idea that the Scots were going to betray him that when a handful of Scottish officers rode up he 'ordered them to go away to a village [probably Daviot] a mile's distance from where he was, and he would send his orders thither'. This rankled with Elcho, who believed Charles Stuart was still concerned only about the Irish and 'neither Spoke to any of the Scots officers present, or inquired after any of the Absent'.

Darkness fell as the Prince followed the Nairn southward, now with only his Irish friends, Sheridan, O'Sullivan and Captain Felix O'Neil (of Irish origin but really a Frenchman), and no more Scots than were absolutely necessary for his safety or as guides. The Scots he retained were Elcho, Aide-de-Camp Alexander MacLeod the Younger of Muiravonside (usually known as 'Sawnie'), a Roman Catholic priest, Father Allan MacDonald, and 'Sawnie's' servant Ned Burke, a North Uist or Skye man who knew the Highlands well. 'Honest Ned', as Forbes called him, stayed with the Prince during much of his travels that summer and, although he could neither read nor write, he was able to recount many details about their travels. After the rising he became a sedan-chair carrier in Edinburgh.

It must have been a hard ride as the river valley climbed steadily and the mountains to the east grew wilder and higher, and at Aberarder, where the Nairn turns eastwards into the Monadhliath Mountains, the fugitives followed the path into Stratherrick, a valley parallel to Loch Ness, but a mile or two to the east of the great long loch. This was Clan Fraser country, the best part of 20 miles from Culloden, and at this distance from the day's disaster Prince Charlie's spirits began to rise. Late in the evening he arrived at Gorthlick, about a mile north of the present-day village of Errogie.

Today Gorthlick is a handsome, square-faced, white farmhouse set in a well-tended garden, located in an elevated position above the main road. The only reminder that it was the Prince's first resting place is a first-floor window at the rear, facing on to the farmyard, which is pointed out as being one from which the Prince escaped. If this story is true it means that the Prince's departure from Gorthlick must have been more precipitate than anyone has admitted to — or perhaps it is simply confused with the tale of his escape at Moy Hall a couple of months earlier. In 1746 Lord Lovat's 'doer' (land factor) lived at Gorthlick, and here the Prince met Simon Fraser, Lord Lovat, chief of Clan Fraser – the one and only time their paths crossed. That night Simon Fraser treated Charles to a fine example of his ability to face in two directions: at seventy-nine years of age he remained as treacherous as ever. He had given his support to the 'King over the Water' in the '45 only after the Prince's first major victory at Prestonpans made a Stuart restoration appear probable, and although he himself was too old to fight and his heir also managed to miss Culloden, he left it to a twenty-year-old lad, Charles Fraser of Inverallochie, to lead his clansmen. Poor Inverallochie was shot in cold blood by one of 'Hangman' Hawley's men as he lay wounded on the battlefield. Although he professed to be a life-long Jacobite, Lord Lovat was never to be trusted.

At Gorthlick Ned Burke said Charlie drank three glasses of wine with Lovat and ate the first food he had had that day: at the end of the abortive night attack on Cumberland all that could be found at Culloden House was a little whisky and bread, and by the time a meal was cooked for him in the morning he was in too great a hurry to get to the battlefield to pause to eat it. Now he enjoyed Lord Lovat's food and wine, and with it

17–26 April. Charlie's route through the remote West Highlands to Loch nan Uamh, where his great adventure had begun only nine months before.

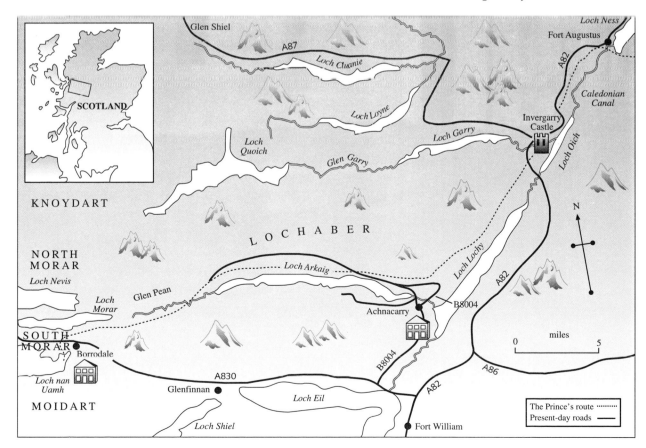

Gorthlick House in Stratherrick. Prince Charlie rested here and met the notorious old Lord Lovat, the only time the two ever came together.

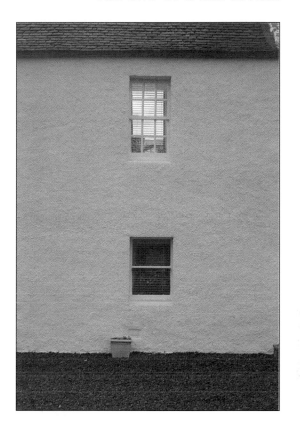

Gorthlick House. Local tradition claims that the Prince escaped by this upper window, but there is no record of a hasty departure from the house. Perhaps this legend is borrowed from his flight from Moy House in his nightclothes some weeks earlier to escape an ambush by Lord Loudoun's men.

Stratherrick, above Fort Augustus. Darkness and lashing rain added to the Prince's difficulties as he rode towards Fort Augustus, through mountainous country pitted with treacherous bogs, burns and little lochs. Ever present was the fear that the Duke of Cumberland's search parties might be in pursuit.

digested some of his host's dubious advice. Elcho believed that the clansmen ought to take to the hills and wage a cat-and-mouse campaign until they were ready to fight again, and old Fraser supported this plan at first. 'Remember how your ancestor Robert Bruce was defeated eleven times before he finally won the Scottish Crown at Bannockburn,' he told the Prince, 'but then turned all his own arguments on their head to express doubts as to whether a mountain campaign could be sustained'. Fraser claimed that while this argument was going on, Charles broke down and wept. 'My good lord,' the Prince cried, 'we are all ruined; I am heart-broken for the misfortunes that beset the poor land of Scotland.' Then he fell into a faint, or so Lovat said.

Elcho was disgusted with Sheridan and his Irish cronies when they sided with Lovat, and Charles himself, obviously in better spirits again, proposed that he should make for MacDonald country in the west until they could establish whether a campaign among the mountains might be viable. If the clan chiefs agreed to fight on, then he would sail to France to bring back money and arms from King Louis.

O'Sullivan later wrote a badly spelled account of the decision to return to France:

'Well,' sayd the Prince, 'I see as well as yu yt my scituation is desperate; I'l make the best of my way to Arisaig. Il be there in Clenranolds Contry & near Locheil, far from Forte William, altogether out of the way of the enemy at least for some time. Il soon know if my friends can undertake any thing at least to guarde their Contry. If they are, Il joyn them, & as there is no mony, without wch it is impossible to keep together or subsist, if they promise to keep out, Il go my self to France to see & bring them Succor of money and men, I hope my presence will do morre with the King then any body I can send.'

At Gorthlick 'Sawnie' MacLeod was ordered to write to Ewan MacPherson of Cluny telling him that they would rally at Fort Augustus, and not at Ruthven in Badenoch as had been mooted before Culloden, but never actually confirmed, largely because Charles Stuart could not contemplate defeat. This letter began, 'You have [heard] no doubt ere now of the ruffle we met with this forenoon. We have suffered a good deal; but hope we shall soon pay Cumberland in his own Coin.' Charles' spirits had rallied sufficiently for the terrible defeat to be thought of as nothing more than a 'ruffle'. His order was absolutely clear: 'We are to review to-morrow [Thursday April 17] at Fort Augustus, the Frasers, Camerons, Stuarts, Clanranald's, and Keppoch's people. His R.H. expects your people will be with us at furthest Friday morning [the 18th]. Dispatch is the more necessary that his Highness has something in view which will make

On the River Garry close to Invergarry Castle the guide, Ned Burke, found a couple of salmon in a net, and cooked them to make the first real meal the Prince had eaten in two days. 'The meat was reckoned very savoury and acceptable,' Ned said afterwards.

Fort Augustus, at the southern end of Loch Ness, was taken by the Jacobites shortly before Culloden, and the Prince ordered his defeated Army to rally here. Instead of waiting, however, he made for the west coast to find a ship to France. The barracks, built in the town at the time of the 1715 rising, was destroyed, and the Caledonian Canal, seen here, was completed a century later.

ample amends for this day's ruffle.' For a second time the defeat was dismissed as a mere 'ruffle', and Charles emphasised his intention of fighting back by adding, 'For God's sake make haste to join us, and bring with you all the people [who] can possibly be brought together. Take care in particular of Lumisden and Sheridan, as they carry with them the Sinews of War.' Andrew Lumisden, a trusted follower, and old Tom Sheridan had the Prince's remaining monies with them.

It has been suggested that this order was nothing more than a piece of disinformation to confuse Cumberland's spies – a blind to give the Prince time to reach the west coast, make contact with a French ship and sail away to safety. But this seems out of character with the way Prince Charlie's mind worked; he was not a coward who would cold-heartedly abandon the Highlanders to save his own skin, as was suggested at the time and since. As for the Fort Augustus rendezvous, that is more likely to have been a result of Lovat's muddled advice, his own confused state of mind at the time, ignorance of the country or simply impetuosity.

Cumberland's search parties could travel as fast as the Prince, so after no more than three hours' sleep, Charles was on his way down Stratherrick to Fort Augustus at the southern end of Loch Ness, the fort whose capture

Loch Lochy. Here the fugitive Prince came to within only a few miles of the Hanoverian stronghold of Fort William, so he turned westward towards Achnacarry in Cameron country, where he knew he would find friends to protect him.

Invergarry Castle. Cumberland's vengeful hunters ensured that only stark walls and empty windows remained of Invergarry Castle, south of Fort Augustus. Charles rested at Invergarry on the day following Culloden. He had stayed at this Glengarry MacDonnell stronghold at the start of the rising, but now found it deserted and awaiting its fate.

was one of his successes in the lead-up to Culloden. Without pausing longer than it took to remove the musket ball which had struck his horse's neck during the battle, he rode on to Invergarry Castle, where he arrived at about two in the morning. Here the resourceful Ned Burke found a couple of salmon trapped in nets and prepared an excellent meal, the best the Prince had enjoyed in forty-eight hours. Afterwards Charles rested at Invergarry until the middle of the following afternoon.

When he had rested, the Prince continued down the Great Glen, following the west side of Loch Lochy, still guided by Ned Burke and accompanied by O'Sullivan and Father Allan MacDonald. At the mouth of Glen Mallie they turned westward close to Cameron of Lochiel's house at Achnacarry, but it was too dangerous to stop there, so they continued along the north shore of Loch Arkaig into the narrow defile of Glen Pean, where they sheltered at a house belonging to Donald Cameron of Glen Pean. From there scouts were sent out to discover whether the clansmen were mustering at Fort Augustus as ordered, but Charles must have lost patience or panicked because, without waiting, he was soon pushing his way westwards towards the greater remoteness of Morar. The country soon turned wilder and the hills higher, making it too difficult for horses, so the journey became a long hard trek on foot. They walked and stumbled on through the night in near pitch darkness since the moon – if they could see it at all on that wet April night – was only in its first quarter. By the morning of 18 April they reached the braes of Morar in the vicinity of Loch Meoble to the south of Loch Morar, Britain's deepest loch. There Angus MacEachain, son-in-law of John MacDonald of Borrodale, found them 'a small sheal house near a wood' where they could rest, for the Prince was utterly worn out. Here he could relax for he was among his good MacDonald friends.

In spite of the 'ruffle' at Culloden the clan grapevine remained in excellent working order. Cluny received 'Sawnie' MacLeod's letter ordering the muster at Fort Augustus the day after it was written, and had shown it to Lord George Murray before the Prince reached Loch Meoble. Murray had already learned that Charles was making for Clan Donald country, and understood at once what was afoot. Beside himself with anger that the Prince was deserting them, he turned the letter over and scrawled savagely on the back:

> Dear Sir, Mr McLeod's letter seems to be a state of politiks I do not comprehend, tho' I can guess it is wrote the day of the Battle; and, instead of sending any word to us, every body are ordered from Lochaber to Badenoch to cover H.R.H. from being pursued, which I wish it had taken effect. Adieu. I wish we may soon see better times.
>
> Your's, G.M.

Ruthven Barracks in Badenoch. The Jacobites believed the rallying place in the event of defeat was to be Ruthven, but arrived there only to be told there was to be no rallying.

The words 'to cover H.R.H. from being pursued' demonstrate how obsessed Murray was by the thought that the Prince was abandoning them. He emphasised this point by adding a bitter little postscript in which he observed that Charles, having proposed a muster at Fort Augustus, did not wait there long enough to meet the clansmen who obeyed his instruction: 'I observe the rendezvous was to be as yesterday at Fort Augustus, but those who came from that last night, say H.R.H. was gone for Clanronald's [sic] country.'

To add insult to his deep hurt, old Tom Sheridan's nephew Michael Sheridan arrived, commanded by the Prince to collect money Charles had given to Aeneas MacDonald at the Ford of Faillie for distribution among his needy followers. 'It is a very hard case that the Prince carries away the

The Dark Mile. The dense woods stretching from Loch Lochy to Loch Arkaig provided welcome refuge in contrast to the bare, exposed hillsides on which the Prince spent much of his time sheltering. The woods overhanging the rough track, which gave rise to its name, were much denser in 1746, and Charles found at least half a dozen hiding places in the area during his flight, among them a hollow tree and caves.

money while so many gentlemen who have sacrificed their fortunes for him are starving,' Lord George exclaimed. 'Damn it!' he added, 'If I had ten guineas in the world I'd with all my heart and soul share it with them.'

Murray had reached Ruthven in Badenoch on 17 April, where he was joined by the Duke of Perth, Lord John Drummond, a few other chiefs and some 1,500 Highlanders. They were a ragged, disorganised, dispirited, leaderless lot, apart from the MacPherson and Ogilvy regiments, which had escaped with light casualties. Elcho, who had been present at Gorthlick during the discussion with Lord Lovat, had expected the campaign to continue among the mountains until the Jacobite Army was ready to face Cumberland again, and so had Lord George Murray, but both now realised they were without supplies, officers or their Prince.

Bitter about the terrible casualties his clansmen of the Atholl Brigade had suffered because of O'Sullivan's disposition of the Jacobite Army, and now white-hot over the Prince's apparent betrayal, Murray sat down and dashed off a long letter to Charles. He poured out his anger, first against the foolhardiness and incompetence that had characterised the rising from beginning to end, then about the Prince's choice of leaders. He berated Charles for sailing to Scotland without French help: 'It was surely wrong to sett up the Royal Standard without having posetive [*sic*] assurance from his most Christian Majesty that he would assist you with all his might,' he raged. But he saved his most vicious censure for the organisation of the campaign, damning Charles' choice of O'Sullivan as Adjutant-General and for placing Hay of Restalrig in charge of supplies. 'Happy had it been for us that Mr O'Sullivan had never got any other charge or office in our Army than the care of the Bagage & equipages, which I'm told he had been brought up to & understood'. As for Hay, he 'served yr R.H. most egregious ill', with the result that the Army was starving and short of equipment when it faced Cumberland. 'Had our feeld of Batle been right choise, & if we had got plenty of provisions, in all Human probability we would have done by the Enemy as they have unhappily done by us.' After such a tirade there was nothing left to the Lieutenant-General but to resign his commission, and that he did.

According to Chevalier de Johnstone's *A Memoir of the Forty-Five*, those who mustered at Ruthven arrived in good enough spirits considering the terrible mauling they had received and were anxious to regroup and retaliate. They waited, but instead of the Prince appearing, 'Sawnie' MacLeod arrived with a curt message from their leader, 'Let every man seek his safety in the best way he can.' Two days later a second letter from the Prince confirmed that it was now every man for himself:

When I came to this Country it was my only view to do all in my power for your good and safety. Alas! I see with grief, I can at present do little for you on this side of the water, for the only thing that can now be done, is to defend your selves till the French assist you. To effectuate this, the only way is to assemble in a body as soon as possible, and then take measures for the best, which you that know the Country are only Judges of. This makes me be of little use here, whereas by my going into France instantly, however dangerous it be, I will certainly engage the French Court either to assist us effectually, and powerfully, or at least to procure you such terms as you would not obtain otherways. My presence there, I flatter myself, will have more effect to bring this sooner to a determination than anybody else.

The letter was read out by Lord George Murray before the clansmen were dismissed to return – as best they could – to their homes. Chevalier de Johnstone described the moment: 'Our separation at Ruthven was truly affecting. We bade one another an eternal adieu. No one could tell whether the scaffold would not be his fate. The Highlanders gave vent to their grief in wild howlings and lamentations; the tears flowed down their cheeks when they thought that their country was now at the discretion of the Duke of Cumberland, and on the point of being plundered; whilst they and their children would be reduced to slavery, and plunged, without resource into a state of remediless distress.'

'Bring it to a determination' the Prince had written. The first news their comrades brought of Cumberland's soldiers' cruelties on the battlefield had already confirmed the only 'determination' Cumberland envisaged, and the Highlanders believed their Prince was abandoning them to that fate. The common men had nowhere to go but home to await their fate, but there was a choice for the chiefs: some returned to their clan lands, but many sailed away to safety in exile.

Lord George Murray returned to his home country of Atholl where he hid in the vast woodlands of Glen Lyon, but the Duke of Perth was too ill to skulk in the hills, so he and his brother Lord John Drummond made their way to the coast in the hope of finding a ship to take them to

Overleaf: Loch Arkaig. The Prince rode along the north side of Loch Arkaig on the day after Culloden. At the western end of the loch the pattern of his flight changed as he reached Glen Pean and the precipitous bare mountains that led into Morar. He now had to walk because the terrain was too difficult for horses. It was in this area that the 'Loch Arkaig Treasure', money brought from France too late to help his campaign, was hidden.

Achnasaul waterfall. This dramatic cataract, between Cameron of Lochiel's house at Achnacarry and Loch Arkaig, lies close to the hiding place where Lochiel's brother discovered Charles and took him to Ben Alder in Badenoch, where the Cameron chief was hiding.

France. Lord Elcho, too, angry and disillusioned with the Prince's conduct at Faillie and Gorthlick, headed for the coast and exile.

There were still men among the Prince's leaders, however, who continued to hold out hopes for renewing the fight with or without him, but Charles had struck a devastating blow against his own Cause. All that can be said in his favour is that he thought that by leaving and saving his own life he was doing the right thing to preserve the dynasty he had been chosen by divine right to lead one day, and that if he stayed in Scotland he might be captured and the Stuart line would be extinguished. Better to leave now and return reinforced than to stay and risk annihilation.

As Charles planned his escape some of his remaining faithful followers were gathering only a few miles away, at the head of Loch Arkaig, among them Donald Cameron of Lochiel. Lochiel's family believed that he had been killed at Culloden until he arrived home at Achnacarry unannounced, carried by his clansmen who had snatched him from the battlefield, with both ankles broken. Lochiel made the painful journey slung across the back of a horse, yet he arrived at Loch Arkaig with neither spirit nor enthusiasm for the Cause diminished. He went into hiding with his brother Dr Archibald Cameron and John Murray of Broughton, the Prince's Secretary, who had come to Cameron country in search of Lochiel and other survivors likely to help him to revive the campaign. In their hide-out close to Loch Arkaig, Lochiel and Murray of Broughton discussed how they might bring the chiefs together to plan a new campaign, but unfortunately they arrived too late to intercept the Prince and talk sense into his head about his future and that of the rising.

On the night of Sunday 20 April Charles' party set out on another difficult night walk, southward this time, through Glenbeasdale to Borrodale House close to the shore of Loch nan Uamh, where the great adventure had begun. In the very room in which he had tried to persuade the clan chiefs to join him the previous summer he now had very different matters to talk over with his Clan Donald friends – how he might escape to France.

FLIGHT TO THE ISLES

Prince Charlie remained at Borrodale for six tense days. From 21 to 26 April the tide of argument ebbed and flowed as clansmen returning from Culloden brought news of enemy movements, and his guardians debated how he might be taken to safety. All the clan leaders were aware that it could only be a matter of time before the government began to comb Morar and Moidart just as they were at present searching glens farther north. And while Loch nan Uamh was difficult to reach from Fort William, it remained vulnerable to attack from the sea – as Captain John Ferguson, one of the Royal Navy's most efficiently ruthless captains, demonstrated only a fortnight after Prince Charlie's stay when he sailed his ship HMS *Furnace* into the loch and burned Borrodale House to the ground.

At this time the Navy presented a far greater danger to the Prince than the Army. Scouts reported increased naval activity in Hebridean waters as the British Navy stepped up its search for fleeing rebels or French rescue ships. Kinlochmoidart's brother the Paris banker Aeneas MacDonald had sailed to Barra recently, and he reported that it took all the skill and seamanship of his boatman Donald MacLeod, and a modicum of luck as well, to evade capture because 'the sea was swarming with sloops of war, boats and yawls full of militia'.

On land Cumberland's destruction quickly spread throughout the Highlands into the mountains west of the Great Glen. Before Culloden the government had decided that clan power must be destroyed once and for all, and Cumberland set about implementing this in a manner that, in today's terminology, was nothing short of ethnic cleansing. The defeat on Drummossie Moor broke the clan system for ever as chiefs turned from paternal guardians of their clansmen and women into mere landlords as greedy as any English landowner or Lowland laird. Highlanders were left with neither the means nor the spirit to win a living from their land, and many emigrated, while others were recruited into the British Army, where they became some of the finest soldiers the Hanoverians could have had to build their empire. In later years many were driven off their crofts to be replaced by sheep, which yielded a better return to the landowners, and by the nineteenth century Highlanders were emigrating in their thousands to build

THE FLIGHT OF BONNIE PRINCE CHARLIE

America, Canada, Australia, New Zealand and every part of the British Empire.

Cumberland was helped in his hunt for the Prince and rebels by militia regiments raised by certain clan chiefs, among them the Campbells, who had never supported the Stuarts, the Sleat MacDonalds and MacLeods of Dunvegan in Skye. Wherever redcoats and black-jacketed militiamen went they left devastation behind: anyone concealing arms was shot out of hand, women were raped and families murdered or driven further into the bleak hills to starve. Homes were burned to the ground, belongings and implements destroyed and cattle driven away. In short, the Highlanders were left without any livelihood.

For King George's Army smoking out rebels in the empty, eerie glens was a frightening experience: here they had no friends and were always open to ambush by clansmen who knew how to fight in mountainous terrain. They were unsure, unsafe and filled with 'hypochondriacal melancholy', which had the effect for making them more vicious in their 'cleansing' of the glens. Cumberland felt as miserable and isolated as his soldiers, and complained bitterly that he reckoned himself 'more in an enemys country' here than when he was warring against the French in Flanders.

The weather became a common foe. Bitter winds swept sleet and rain across the mountains day after day during April, and the nights remained freezing cold right into May. The summer of 1746 was little better. Redcoat hunters often felt as miserable, cold and hungry in their makeshift shelters in the glens as their quarry were, lying in mountain hide-outs. Major-General John Campbell of Mamore, who had charge of the Clan Campbell militia out searching alongside government soldiers, once complained that his pursuit of rebels was hampered by storms that had raged for three days without abating. One night, as the Earl of Loudoun sat down to prepare a report, he had to hand the pen over to one of his officers after writing only a few words – his fingers were too numb to hold it.

While Cumberland concentrated on the area around Inverness during the weeks immediately after Culloden, Campbell of Mamore was desperate to send his men across Loch Linnhe into the heart of Ardgour, Morar and Moidart, where he felt certain the Prince and rebel leaders would be found. As soon as news of Culloden reached him he wrote to the Duke: 'I propose to scour the western islands, from which I think the rebells (as being the most rational rout[e]) will attempt getting out of Britain', but the Duke was too busy in Inverness to send help.

Campbell and his spies had one great advantage over Lowlanders and English soldiers: they knew the country well, and spoke Gaelic so they could easily pass themselves off as sympathetic fellow clansmen. As a result, Mamore always remained remarkably well informed of the Prince's movements, with only one limitation – information usually took a week to ten days to reach him, by which time Prince Charlie was on his way to a new hide-out. This saved the Prince time and time again, and greatly frustrated King George's search parties. Credit must also be given to Highlanders, for even though the reward of £30,000 was still on offer none betrayed him.

If proof were needed of the danger Prince Charlie's life was in throughout that summer, it was provided by Alexander MacDonald of Kingsburgh, who was held prisoner in Fort Augustus. A fair-haired, young Highlander named Roderick MacKenzie had allowed his redcoat captors to believe he was the Prince and was murdered, and his head was brought into the fort by his murderers, no doubt in the hope of earning them the £30,000 reward. They asked Kingsburgh, who had met Prince Charles, if he would recognise the head of the Young Pretender if he saw it.

'I would know the head very well,' Kingsburgh replied, 'provided it were upon the body.'

The memorial to Roderick MacKenzie.

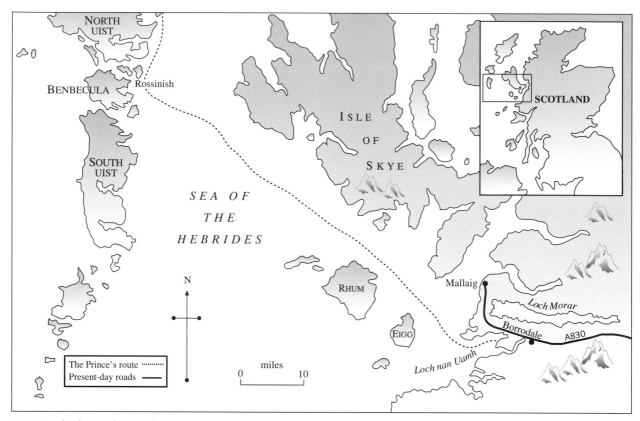

26–9 April. The perilous night journey to the Outer Hebrides ended at Rossinish, Benbecula.

'What if the head be not upon the body? Do you think you could know it in that case?'

Kingsburgh replied, 'In that case, Sir, I will not pretend to know anything about it.' And that was the end of the matter.

As the days passed clan leaders at Borrodale realised it was unsafe for Charles to remain in Morar hoping for a ship to arrive from France: far better to take him to the relative safety of the Outer Hebrides and find some means of spiriting him out of Scotland from there. But Charles as usual had his own ideas, and announced a hare-brained plan to throw himself on the mercy of one of the two great Skye chiefs, Sir Alexander MacDonald of Sleat or Norman MacLeod of MacLeod – the very men who had refused to join him at the start of the rising and whose militia regiments were now participating in the hunt.

The clan leaders who were with him persuaded Charles to sail instead to the Outer Hebrides, where there were so many islands, indented with thousands of little creeks and sealochs, that it would be relatively easy to find a hiding place. And who better to take him there than the old sea dog Donald MacLeod, who had spent his life sailing in these waters and knew them better then anyone. Donald hailed from Gualtergill, near Dunvegan in Skye, and was one of the Laird of MacLeod's clansmen, but there was no ambiguity about where his loyalties lay. No one was quite certain where he might be found, however, so at least three messengers were sent to scour the country for him. He was soon tracked down and asked to come to Borrodale to take the Prince to safety. He did not hesitate.

Donald MacLeod later recounted his adventures as the Prince's guardian with gusto to Bishop Robert Forbes for inclusion in *The Lyon in Mourning*, and who is to blame him. He was well aware of the importance of his role in the Prince Charlie legend and did not spoil his tale in telling it. He made the Prince talk to him like an old friend, and in return gave his advice as bluntly as a father or one of those Scottish commanders whose frankness caused such offence during the campaign. It is interesting that Charles, who usually tolerated contradiction from no one, accepted this, and it is indicative of the old man's easy relationship with the Prince that he was not overawed by Charles' royal status. He could never manage to get his royal charge's rank right either, at times addressing him as 'Your Majesty' and at others 'Excellency'. And Charles answered to both.

More than a year later Donald MacLeod showed great emotion when recounting the details of his first meeting with the Prince. Bishop Forbes said the old seaman 'grat sare, the tears came running down his cheeks'. Donald was alone in the woods at Borrodale when the Prince approached him. 'Are you Donald MacLeod of Gualtergill in Skye?' Charles asked.

'I am the same man, may it please your Majesty, at your service. What is your pleasure wi' me?' Donald replied.

'You see, Donald, I am in distress. I therefore throw myself into your bosom, and let you do with me what you like. I hear you are an honest man, and fit to be trusted.' This was the point at which Donald wept.

'Alas, may it please your excellency, what can I do for you, for I am but a poor auld man, and can do very little for myself?'

When Charles asked if he would take letters to the Chief of Sleat and the Laird of MacLeod, Donald's tears turned into a torrent of accusation against the two who at that moment had men searching not 12 miles away. The tirade ended with a fatherly, but firm, 'Na, you mauna do it.'

The Prince capitulated. 'I hear, Donald, you are a good pilot; that you know all this coast well, and therefore I hope you can carry me safely through the islands where I may look for more safety than I can do here.'

By Saturday 26 April the old seaman had found an eight-oared boat and brought it to Loch nan Uamh, crewed by Ned Burke and seven clansmen, among them his own son, a lad of fifteen, who had run away to fight for Charlie at Culloden. As they were about to leave, Donald's seaman's eye saw a storm approaching so he proposed that they should wait, but Charles would have none of it. Perhaps the old man's warning about Sleat and MacLeod militia patrols had put such fear into him that he was determined to be off the mainland as soon as possible, or perhaps he was just reverting to his old persona of prince of the royal blood who must be obeyed without question. Another factor that would make for

CLAN DONALD AND PRINCE CHARLIE

Prince Charlie would have been captured but for the unfailing loyalty of many clans – Camerons, MacKinnons, MacPhersons and especially the MacDonalds. He rarely felt secure when separated from them or outside their clanlands, and four of his five months in hiding were spent in their company.

Clan Donald, the Great Clan, had ruled large tracts of the Highlands stretching from the hills of Lochaber to Skye and the Outer Hebrides for centuries, and many of the chiefs were Jacobites – Barisdale, Belfinlay, Glencoe, Glengarry, Keppoch, Lochgarry, Scotus and Tiendrich among them. Others, who did not commit themselves to the rising in 1745, proved to be good friends while the Prince was in flight. Sir Alexander MacDonald, Chief of Sleat, raised a militia regiment for the government, yet he and the Duke of

Background: The majestic red Cuillins from Loch Cill Chriosd, south Skye.

Sir Alexander MacDonald of Sleat.

Ormiclett, home of the Claranald MacDonald chief, was burned down during the '15 rising.

MacDonald of Borrodale's house by Loch nan Uamh, where Prince Charlie rallied the clans.

Cumberland never trusted one another. On first meeting Sleat, Cumberland asked half-jokingly, 'Is this the great rebel of the Isles?'

'No, my Lord Duke,' Sleat replied, 'had I been the Rebel of the Isles, your Royal Highness would never have crossed the Spey.'

Clanranald, the other great Clan Donald chief who hedged his bets, held the islands of Uist and Benbecula and part of Morar on the mainland. While he remained at home, his son Young Clanranald fought for the Prince and helped in the escape.

Alongside their chiefs, Alexander MacDonald of Kingsburgh, Flora, his guide to Skye, 'One-eyed Hugh' of Armadale, Donald Roy, Sleat militiamen on unofficial 'leave' from their companies and scores of unnamed clansmen and women helped to ferry Prince Charlie among the islands and guide him beyond his pursuers. Collectively they were the folk who made the escape possible.

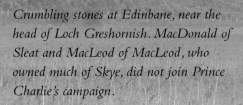

Crumbling stones at Edinbane, near the head of Loch Greshornish. MacDonald of Sleat and MacLeod of MacLeod, who owned much of Skye, did not join Prince Charlie's campaign.

Nunton on Benbecula. By chance the Prince landed in the Outer Hebrides close to the home of the Clanranald chief.

urgency was the fact that 26 April was a Saturday and if they sailed that night the militia and redcoats would be too busy with sabbath day prayers in the morning to maintain a strict vigil on the Sea of the Hebrides. For whatever reason, Charles Stuart was determined to leave without delay, taking with him O'Sullivan, Felix O'Neil and Father Allan MacDonald.

With Donald at the helm and the Prince seated at his feet they pushed off from shore in the gloaming, but before they were far out into the loch the storm blew up just as the old seaman had predicted – the loch turned rough and rain and wind beat into them as thunder and lightning rolled overhead. The Prince begged to be put ashore – anywhere, even on the loch shore where high waves were smashing against the rocks. MacLeod refused, and made for open water. 'Since we are here,' he told the Prince, 'we have nothing for it but, under God, to set out to sea directly. Is it not as good for us to be drown'd in clean water as to be dashed in pieces upon a rock and to be drowned too?'

After that there was 'hush and silence' and the men rowed against the strong wind out of Loch nan Uamh and the Sound of Arisaig, then raised a sail and set a course north-westward into the pitch darkness of open sea. The small vessel was tossed violently as she made her way through the channel that separates the islands of Eigg and Rum from Skye with neither compass, lamp nor pump to empty water out of the boat. Donald claimed the Prince's spirits remained high even though he was 'more or less under a bloody flux' throughout the voyage, presumably meaning he was seasick. With relief 'peep of day' revealed the Long Island off their port bow, although the storm had blown them well to the north of their intended destination.

They were close to the coast of Benbecula, which lies between North and South Uist, and there they landed with difficulty at Rossinish, an uninhabited rocky promontory on the north-east coast. They had been at sea for eight hours, and wind and rain were still beating into them as they

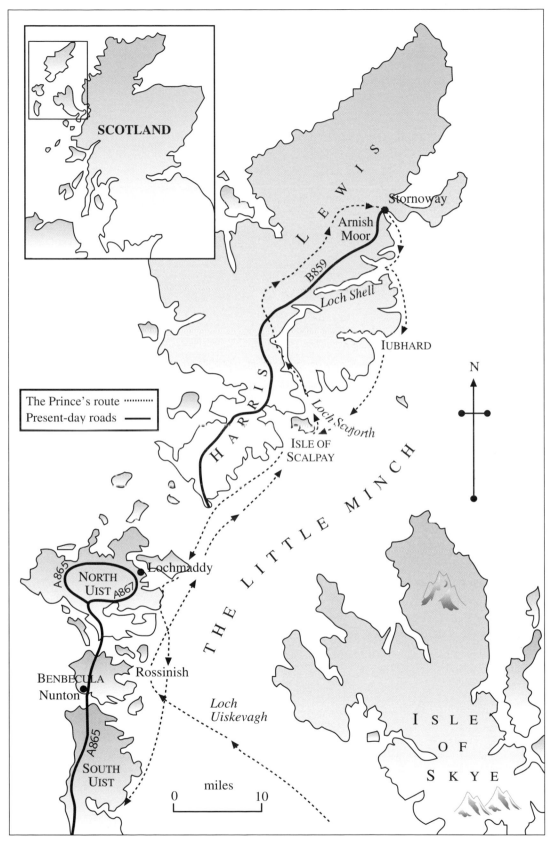

The Prince's route ···········
Present-day roads ——————

29 April–11 May. Rossinish to Stornoway and back to South Uist.

Rossinish. The boat carrying Charles from the mainland to the Outer Hebrides was blown off course by gales, and he landed on these bare rocks at Rossinish on the north-east corner of Benbecula, further north than his intended destination.

hauled their boat on to land and found an uninhabited hut in which they were able to make a fire to dry their clothes. Everyone, the Prince included, was wet to the skin so an old sail was spread on the bare ground for Charles to sleep on while his clothes dried. As he slept his companions found and killed a cow and boiled some of the beef in a pot Donald had prudently brought with him in the boat. With plenty of meat and nobody to disturb them they stayed at this hut for two days and two nights.

Although Rossinish was remote and uninhabited it lay only 6 miles or so from MacDonald of Clanranald's house. The Chief came to the Prince with 'a sute of new Highland cloaths', and for the first time it appears Charles put on the kilt. In spite of Victorian artist John Pettie's splendid portrayal of him in full Highland dress at Holyrood (see p. 4) there is no evidence that he wore the kilt during the campaign. An eyewitness at one of his Edinburgh levees referred to tartan and 'Highland dress' worn with breeches, and a Hanoverian spy described these as matching his tartan waistcoat. The West Highland Museum at Fort William has a pair of trews in a dull red tartan – certainly not Royal Stuart – reputedly worn by the Prince in Scotland. To ride out to review his troops in camp near Edinburgh he dressed in a blue jacket and red cloth trousers, but made an impressive entrance into Glasgow in crimson velvet breeches. Nowhere is there mention of a kilt until he landed on the Long Island, and then he put it on in order to appear less conspicuous. At least three fragments of this kilt survive, one in the New Museum of Scotland in Edinburgh, one in the West Highland Museum and the third at Stoneyhurst College. He took to this new dress, which was ideal for clambering among mountains and sleeping rough, and wore the kilt during most of the remainder of his flight. Clanranald brought to the Prince Neil MacEachain, a young man who had trained for the priesthood at Douai and spoke French and Gaelic. Quiet and self-effacing, Neil proved to be the most underestimated character in the drama of the Prince's escape. He never talked grandly of his exploits and after the adventure was over returned to France, where he adopted the name MacDonald. His son became one of Napoleon's generals and a marshal of France.

Another who learned of the Prince's movements in the Long Island, and made trouble, was the South Uist Presbyterian minister, the Reverend John MacAulay. The minister, whose grandson was the Victorian historian Lord Macaulay, was no friend of the Stuarts and soon sent word of the Young Pretender's presence on the Long Island to the government searchers.

By one of those ironies of history, only a couple of days after Charles left the mainland two French ships sailed into Loch nan Uamh and dropped anchor. They arrived with orders to bring the Prince back should he be in need of rescue – a remarkable instruction since news of the disaster of Culloden had not yet reached Paris and would not do so until nearly the middle of May. The man with the 'second sight' to arrange this was the faithful Antoine Walsh, the privateer who had brought the Prince to Scotland the previous year, and kept a close watch on the progress of the campaign through the winter and spring of 1745–6.

Alarm bells rang when Walsh learned of the Jacobite retreat into the Highlands in February, and realising the campaign was in deep, deep trouble, he sent a memorandum to the Navy Minister in Paris suggesting that no more men should be sent to Scotland until there was better news of the campaign. He proposed, however, that two privateers should be dispatched to Scotland quickly with money and arms, but also with instructions to bring 'le Prince Edouard' back to France if he could no longer hold out in Scotland. Walsh tried to sound optimistic in his note by adding, 'It could well be that, before the ships reach him, the Prince's cause will have revived'. But these were not the words of a hopeful man.

With permission granted, two ships, the *Mars* and *Bellone*, were fitted out and dispatched to Scotland. They anchored in Loch nan Uamh on the second to last day of April to be greeted by a ragged group of clansmen, who broke the news of the Culloden defeat and the Prince's flight. By now Captain Ferguson had burned down Borrodale House and the French officers who came ashore were appalled at the terrible conditions in which they found the Highlanders living – this was a taste of the devastation that was being wreaked throughout clan lands. The house the Frenchmen visited was probably a hut in which Aeneas MacDonald of Borrodale lived after his home was destroyed, a single dark, smoke-filled room with the sparsest of furnishings and straw on the ground for beds. The French thought Scottish clansmen desperately primitive.

The French agreed to unload firearms to sustain a summer guerrilla campaign in the hills until the Jacobite Army had time to regroup, and brandy, but hesitated to land several casks of French gold they had also brought because the Prince himself was not present to accept it. Murray of Broughton, as the Prince's former Secretary, persuaded them he had authority to take charge of the gold and it was put ashore.

'Sawney' MacLeod and Sir Thomas Sheridan, who had to be left behind when the Prince sailed to the Outer Hebrides, confirmed that the Prince had made up his mind to return to France and was now on the Long Island, hoping to find some means of leaving Scotland. Lochiel, his brother and Murray of Broughton were bitterly disappointed: to flee to France, said Lochiel, would be 'dishonourable to himself and so harmful to the whole Scottish nation'.

News of the arrival of the *Mars* and *Bellone* travelled fast along the Jacobite and Hanoverian grapevines, and by 1 May Captain Thomas Noel in HMS *Greyhound*, lying at anchor off Isleoronsay in Skye, had word of

The Batle of Loch nan Uamh by Charles Brooking.

their presence. He set off in pursuit the following morning, accompanied by the sloop HMS *Baltimore*, and a second sloop HMS *Terror*, which he was lucky enough to encounter off the island of Eigg. At dawn on the morning of 3 May this little flotilla sailed into Loch nan Uamh just as the Frenchmen were unloading their cargo.

The *Greyhound* went straight into the attack and raked the *Mars*, which had unwisely remained at anchor when the British appeared, so that she was unable to bring all her guns into action. Clansmen on the loch shore had to dodge cannon-balls as they rushed to and fro, hiding the arms, money and gunpowder they had been unloading, and they were so close that at one point the *Greyhound* fired directly at them.

After six hours the British were forced to withdraw to repair their sails, while the *Mars* was left with 3 feet of water in her hold, having taken sixty-five hits above and seven below the water line. With so much damage and twenty-nine of her crewmen dead and eighty-five wounded, the best she and the *Bellone* could do was limp off home.

The Frenchmen took with them the Duke of Perth, who died on the voyage, and Lord John Drummond, contented to abandon the Cause and resume his career as an officer in King Louis' Army. Elcho, who couldn't wait to put as many miles between himself and Charles Stuart as possible, and old Tom Sheridan, now too old for the rebel life, also sailed to France. Lockhart of Carnwath and the inefficient John Hay of Restalrig were also on board. Murray of Broughton and Lochiel chose to remain behind, still hoping to organise a campaign among the mountains.

The final blast of the Battle of Loch nan Uamh – and of Prince Charlie's '45 campaign – came from neither the Royal Navy nor the privateers, but from a lone Highlander busying himself on the shore of Loch nan Uamh to ensure that the brandy would find a good home. He let some lighted embers from his pipe drop into a barrel of gunpowder, blowing himself to kingdom come and sending his fellow clansmen racing for cover.

The casks of gold were hidden in the mountains around Loch Arkaig, and became known as the 'Loch Arkaig Treasure', breeding envy, greed and suspicion among the clans, and quarrelling that reverberated all the way from Lochaber to Rome over many years. It brought the honesty of men like Dr Archibald Cameron and Ewan MacPherson of Cluny into question, and added theft to accusations of betrayal against John Murray of Broughton. The worst villain of all was the man who was least suspected, Alasdair Ruadh Macdonnell, heir to the Chief of Glen Garry. Young Glen Garry not only helped himself to the Loch Arkaig gold, but spied for the British government in return for payment, using the alias 'Pickle the Spy'.

By the time the *Mars* and *Bellone* and Captain Noel's little fleet were licking their wounds after their encounter in Loch nan Uamh a means of escape had been devised for the Prince. He would be taken to Stornoway on the island of Lewis, where he would be passed off as an Orkney

Overleaf: Scalpay. Charles spent several days at a farmhouse on the island of Scalpay, in southern Harris, while his guardians were trying to hire a boat at Stornoway to take him to the Continent. These were carefree days spent fishing with his host's young son.

seaman whose ship had foundered and who now was seeking a vessel to take him home. From Orkney it would be easy to find another boat to carry him to Norway or France.

On the evening of Tuesday 29 April, the day the Frenchmen put into Loch nan Uamh, Donald's seamen relaunched their eight-oared boat at Rossinish and set out under darkness, northwards along the wild coast of North Uist to Scalpay, a small island off the entrance to Loch Seaforth in Harris. They made good time in spite of appalling sailing conditions to reach Scalpay a couple of hours before dawn. Here Donald had a friend, one Donald Campbell, who could be trusted to take care of the Prince while his Orkney voyage was arranged.

O'Sullivan and Charles were passed off as a father and son named Sinclair, and since the fugitive's true identity was not revealed even to Campbell's family, he was able to relax in the guise of plain Mr Sinclair, the shipwrecked sea captain, during his four nights on the island.

He trusted this Campbell family, who were well disposed to him in spite of bearing the name of the clan most opposed to the Stuarts, and Mrs Campbell, who had been born a MacDonald, was especially kind to him. Afterwards she painted a homely domestic picture of him: Charles still needed less sleep than his companions and would wake before anyone else and come and ask Mrs Campbell what was for breakfast, or go foraging in the store cupboard himself to find something to eat. Once he discovered a couple of eggs which he begged her to cook for his breakfast, and she could not refuse him. After breakfast he and the Campbells' son Kenneth would go off fishing together like a pair of boys, chatting happily as they waited for a catch. When they hooked a cod, they brought it home and Charles watched while it was prepared and cooked. One day the pair came upon one of Campbell's cows stuck in a bog and the Prince took his coat off and got mud up to his breeches helping to free it.

Young Kenneth had no idea who Mr Sinclair was, but questioned him about where he had come from and where he was going. The Prince explained that he and his companions were strangers who had been shipwrecked and were in search of a boat to take them home. The Scalpay interlude left a picture of what Charles Stuart's boyhood might have been had he not been a prince.

Leaving the large eight-oared boat behind, Donald borrowed a smaller, six-oared vessel from his friend Campbell to sail to Stornoway, where he was well known and would be able to hire a suitable craft for the voyage to Orkney. It took several days to find a suitable boat and pass the news back to Scalpay, where the Prince was waiting with growing impatience. The moment he learned that a ship had been found at Stornoway, Charles set out to walk the 30 miles to the town, leaving Father Allan MacDonald behind – no loss according to Ned Burke who said the Prince never agreed with the priest and cared little for his company. Charlie was accompanied

Stornoway was the most important port on the Long Island in 1746, as it is today, and Prince Charlie tried to find a boat there to take him to Orkney and back to the Continent.

The head of Loch Seaforth on the island of Harris. One of Charles' companions called the tracks from here to Stornoway the 'worst roads in the world'. Even the guide lost his way and added miles to the journey.

Loch Seaforth, Harris. The calmness of the broad entrance to Loch Seaforth is deceptive: when Charles sailed into the loch on his way from Scalpay to Stornoway his boatmen had to struggle against storms of wind and rain.

On Arnish Moor, close to Stornoway, the fugitives were faced with peatbogs, rocks and burns, which had to be overcome as well as a hostile little 'army' of fearful Stornoway folk.

on the walk to Stornoway by O'Sullivan, O'Neil and a guide who proved so hopeless that he led them 8 miles out of their way. Every yard of their 38-mile walk 'through the worst of roads in the world' had been a struggle against wind and rain and by the time they came within sight of Stornoway the following day they were wet to the skin, shivering and weary.

While they remained huddled on the open moor on the outskirts of the town, they sent the guide into Stornoway to alert Donald to their arrival and to ask him to send them some bread and much-needed brandy.

Donald did better: although Lewis was Clan MacKenzie country — whose chief the Earl of Seaforth had refused to support the rising — he found shelter for the Prince at the home of Mrs MacKenzie of Kildun at Arnish just a mile or two outside the town. MacLeod described Charles' rain-sodden arrival at the house: 'Here the Prince was obliged to throw off his shirt, which one of the company did wring upon the hearth-stone, and did spread it upon a chair before the fire to have it dried.'

Charles, O'Sullivan and O'Neil had only half a dozen shirts between them, and because of the constant unrelenting rain they found that when they stripped off one shirt to dry it the other they were about to put on was just as wet. Nonetheless, according to MacLeod, the Prince's spirits never flagged, no matter the circumstances or how ill he felt. He slept no more than three or four hours at a stretch, and each morning drank a cup of cold water at a draught. In his pocket he carried a little bottle from which he took a few drops of a mysterious potion from time to time and declared it an excellent cure for every ill.

MacLeod returned to Stornoway to find MacKenzie sympathy began and ended in Arnish; in the town he was faced with 200 or 300 angry, armed men, called to arms because it was thought he had brought the fugitive Young Pretender to the island with 500 men. 'Has the Devil possessed you?' the astounded boatman demanded. 'Where, I pray you, could the Prince in his present condition get 500 or 100 men together?' The Lewismen had been informed of Charles' arrival by Colin MacKenzie, the Presbyterian teacher on the island, who had it from the Reverend Aulay MacAulay, Presbyterian minister on Harris, who had it from his son, the Presbyterian minister on South Uist.

According to MacLeod, the MacKenzies calmed down on learning that Charles had brought no army, and told him they had no intention of harming the Prince. They were willing to allow Charles to return to the Continent (as islanders called the Scottish mainland in those days), but were too afraid to supply a boat or pilot for the journey — so terrified of Hanoverian vengeance, declared Donald, were they that £500 would not have persuaded them.

Accounts of the Stornoway encounter vary: Donald blamed the MacAulay ministers and schoolmaster MacKenzie for betraying the Prince's presence, a second accused a MacAulay boatman and Ned Burke's version said old Donald 'having got drunk, had told some of his acquaintances [the name of the person] for whom he hired the ship'. Ned also told how he tried to persuade Charles to take to the mountains when the Stornoway 'army' marched out to Arnish, but Charles refused: 'How long is it, Ned, since you turned cowardly?' he asked, and assured Burke that he would take out the best of them if they laid a hand on him. Charles remained calm enough to insist on a good night's rest before he moved. 'Let the consequence be what it would,' said Donald, 'he could not think of stirring anywhere . . . till he should sleep a little, so much was he fatigued with the late tedious journey'.

In the morning they sailed, but without two of their crewmen who had deserted when the Stornoway 'army' approached. They were well provisioned for once since they had slaughtered one of Mrs MacKenzie's cows the day before and took the head and some of the meat with them, as well as some meal, brandy, sugar, bread and 'a junt' of butter which their hostess had given them. Mrs MacKenzie refused payment for the cow, but Donald insisted: 'Deel a man or woman should have it to say that the Prince ate their meat for nought.'

They had gone no more than a mile or two down the wild, loch-pitted Lewis coast when a group of British men-of-war hove in sight off Kebock Head, and sent them rowing like fury for safety on Iubhard, a deserted island at the mouth of Loch Shell that Stornoway fishermen used for drying their fish. Seeing the small boat approach, the fish-curers working on the island fled, believing them to be a press-gang from one of the warships trying to snatch them for service in the Navy. Charles and his companions remained on Iubhard for a total of four nights, with plenty of fish to add to their already well-stocked commissariat. This was a major problem during the Prince's flight – supplies of food were so erratic it was either a case of feast or famine, and now was feasting time.

Ned Burke acted as cook and baker, but sometimes the Prince lent a hand, and caused consternation with his rough and ready, unhygienic methods. On one occasion he and Ned had a long argument about whether some butter they proposed to use for cooking fish was clean or not, but Charles insisted they use it. Even Donald, the old Skye skipper, who must have eaten some strange and none too pure dishes in his day, declined it, but 'they made a very hearty meal of the fish and the crumbs of bread swimming among the butter,' and the Prince declared it 'very nice indeed'. On another occasion on Iubhard, while Ned was baking an oatcake, Charles insisted on incorporating some of the brain of Mrs MacKenzie's cow into the oatmeal. 'When the cake was fully fired the Prince divided it into so many pieces, giving every gentleman a bit of it,' said Donald. 'And it made very good bread indeed.'

Although he was willing to take a hand in the cooking, the Prince did not eat with the common boatmen. They always kept separate tables for the royal party and servants and crewmen. However, he had to share the only shelter on the island, a leaky hut in which the fishermen stayed overnight while curing their catch. The Prince had to sleep on the bare ground and, as rain continued without a break, the boat's sail had to be spread over the roof. In fact the only comfort the fugitives enjoyed on Iubhard was a peat fire, which at least kept them warm.

After the feast of Iubhard, famine followed only a few days later when they found themselves being pursued again. They sailed on Saturday

10 May to continue the voyage to Scalpay, but found Donald Campbell gone because he feared the authorities might find out he had sheltered the Prince the previous week. They now decided to return to Uist, and to make better speed took Campbell's boat, which Charles said was 'a fine, light, swift-sailing thing'. It was as well they took the lighter craft, for the wind had dropped and the crewmen had to row hard all night to make progress until a breeze blew up at daybreak and they were able to hoist a sail. All their fresh water and food had gone except for a little oatmeal, which they had no means of cooking, so it was mixed raw with seawater to turn it into a kind of gruel, known as Drammach. The Prince nobly pronounced the dish 'no bad food', and because he ate it, everybody else had to force it down. He called for a bottle of brandy immediately afterwards and gave everybody, companions and crewman, a well deserved dram.

Their adventures were still not over. As they passed Loch Finsbay, one of the many little inlets and fiords that indent the Harris coast, another British warship loomed astern and gave chase. Telling his tale a year later, Ned claimed that this was the dreaded Captain Ferguson's HMS *Furnace*, but this is not possible because Ferguson did not arrive in Hebridean waters until a week later, on 17 May. However, there were plenty of other

Finsbay, Harris. Bleak hill and dark peatbogs were everywhere, with water underfoot and overhead.

Rodil at the southern tip of Harris. The hundreds of sealochs and little islands on the Harris coast were good friends to the Prince. When pursued at Rodil the boatmen rowed into shallow water where the Royal Navy hunters could not follow.

Royal Navy captains around who could smell Jacobites a mile off. The frigates HMS *Greyhound*, *Baltimore* and *Terror*, which had taken part in the Battle of Loch nan Uamh at the beginning of the month, were joined by the sloop HMS *Raven* just after the *Mars* and *Bellone* left for France. Later this small fleet was joined by HMS *Glasgow*, *Trial*, *Happy Janet* and *Furnace*. It was quite a force – all in search of one man.

Suspicious of this small boat scudding furtively down the Harris coast, the man-of-war gave chase in full sail, but the crafty MacLeod outmanoeuvred her. 'Our little sail was full too,' he recounted. 'He pursued us for three leagues; but we escaped by plying our oars heartily, they being better to us than arms could have been at that time.' Skilfully the old Skye boatman made for shallow water, among rocks, where the large warship could not follow, and out of gun range. 'The water failing the man-of-war, he was not in a condition to pursue farther. We steered upon a point called Rondill [Rodil at the extreme southern end of Harris], when the Prince expressed himself as formerly that he should never be taken in life.'

The warship refused to give up until darkness and an ebb tide allowed Donald to steer into another creek out of reach. After another miserable night at sea he landed the Prince on North Uist, back in friendly MacDonald clanlands, out of sight, yet still almost within the enemy's grasp.

OVER THE SEA TO SKYE

Under cover of darkness the little six-oared boat continued to hug the North Uist coast. For once bad weather was an ally: the wind veered and intensified into a hard gale, driving heavy rain before it and forcing the larger naval ships to head out to sea, or risk being driven on to the rocks. This took them out of firing range of their quarry. By morning Donald MacLeod turned the bow of the boat into Loch Uiskevagh, a broad, shapeless sealoch on Benbecula, close to Rossinish, where the Prince had first arrived on the Long Island. Uiskevagh, like so many lochs on the eastern side of the Outer Hebrides, is wide at its mouth and contains a mass of small islands and rocky inlets, offering safe hiding places. Donald steered for one of these islands where they found a shelter – too primitive even to be called a hut – which offered nothing more than protection from the teeming rain. Ned Burke described how the door was so low that they had to lay heather on the ground to allow the Prince to crawl inside without plastering his clothes in mud.

The party spent three relaxed but busy days there, and again found plenty to nourish them. They fished and shot birds, which Ned declared provided 'very savoury meat', and at low tide one of the oarsmen, wading among the rocks, managed to trap a large partan, which he waved towards the Prince. Charles raced towards him holding out a wooden bowl and playfully asked him to share his catch. The fat crab made an appetising change from their recent diet of gruel formed from salt water and meal. Ned Burke and Donald MacLeod amused the Prince with tricks and nonsense, which he not only took in good part, but actually relished. One day the sole came off Ned's shoe, and the Prince, overhearing him curse the misfortune of having to go barefoot, raised his own foot to reveal that his own sole was missing. For once the garrulous Ned was speechless.

Often during the flight Charles became a very different man from the prince weighed down with worry during the campaign. Round the peat fire in their shelters, he and his companions talked politics, discussed prospects of further help from France, drank toasts or just talked nonsense. Charles defended Louis XV, pointing out that a king and his council were

Loch Uiskevagh, near Rossinish, was a broad sealoch with many inlets and little islands that offered excellent hiding places.

Previous pages: Looking from Benbecula towards North Uist, typical Long Island landscape and seascape, which involved long uncomfortable voyages by boat or treks across bleak wet moorland. Charles coped with both the weather and terrain with remarkably little complaint.

two very different things, and he spoke of hopes of marriage to the French King's second daughter, Princess Henrietta, referred to in toasts only as 'the Black Eye'.

Prince Charlie's spirits did not remain buoyant all the time: alongside playful, carefree episodes there were periods of despair and low spirits, which even brought on illness. The intense week of cat-and-mouse with the British Navy along the Harris and Lewis coast, the threat of the Stornoway armed band and hard living in dreadful conditions everywhere took their toll, so that by the time he reached Loch Uiskevagh his nerves were quite raw. Besides, there were problems to be faced, and he needed advice to help resolve them, but fortunately he was close to Nunton again and able to send for Clanranald.

The chief came immediately, and 'never was a man wolcomer, to be sure' said O'Sullivan. He brought some beer, biscuits, trout and a couple of bottles of Spanish wine, which O'Sullivan proposed to hide away to cheer the Prince in his lower moments. But Charles would have none of it – the wine must be shared among all of them. The chief also sent the Prince a new Highland outfit to replace the one he had given him earlier, but which was now 'tore to pieces and full of soat [soot]'. Charles was delighted with his new clothes and, according to O'Sullivan, leapt about and cried, 'I only want the Itch to be a compleat Highlander.' That was to come in time. Another welcome present from Clanranald was a silver cup, which pleased the Prince greatly because he hated drinking out of the same wooden cog as the rest of the party. But he refused sheets Clanranald proposed to send, saying that, as a Highlander, he needed nothing but his tartan plaid.

Clanranald proposed that Charles should hide on the wild, rocky east coast of South Uist while Donald MacLeod sailed to the mainland with letters to Lochiel and Murray of Broughton to sound out current prospects there and bring back money and much-needed brandy to keep the cold, wet summer at bay.

Donald tracked Cameron and Murray down to their hide-out near the head of Loch Arkaig, but their replies proved to be a bitter disappointment. The Highlands were being devastated and most of the chiefs had either fled abroad or were in hiding, while their clansmen were now so scattered that there could be no prospect of reviving the campaign in the near future. And as for money, although Broughton must have known where the 'Loch Arkaig Treasure' was hidden, he sent nothing. He told Donald he had only about 60 louis d'or, 'which was not worth the while to send'. Charlie might not have agreed, but he had to accept his former secretary's refusal. In fact, MacLeod's only success was in his quest for brandy. Donald laid hands on 2 ankers (about 16 gallons in total) without much difficulty, and brought it back when he returned after spending about eighteen days on the mainland.

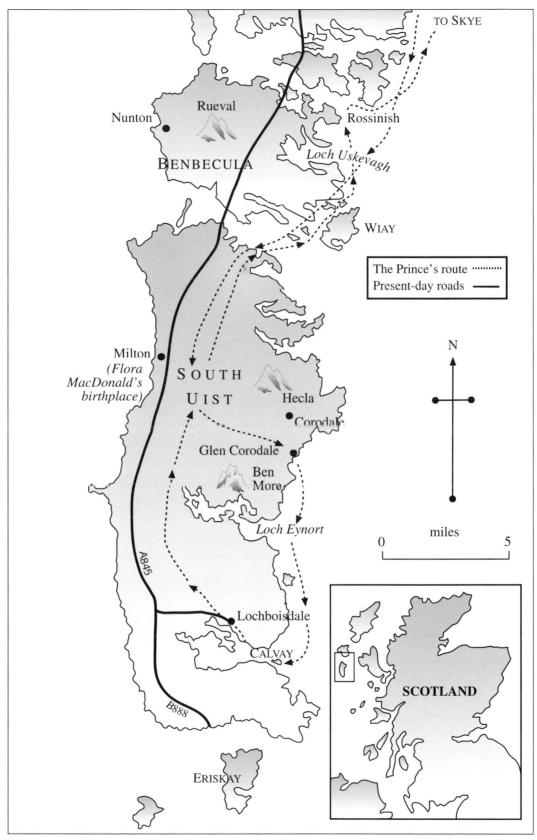

13 May–28 June. To Corodale, Lochboisdale and back to Benbecula and North Uist.

Hecla and Ben More. Between these twin South Uist peaks Charles' guardians found the most comfortable hiding place for him at Corodale, where he spent three idyllic weeks hunting game, talking with chiefs and drinking far into the night.

The meeting with Clanranald also renewed contact with Neil MacEachain, who became the Prince's closest companion and guided him to the new hide-away in a hut at Corodale, a place so inaccessible that it could be reached only by a hard overland hike through the remote glen between Hecla and Ben More, a pair of mountains nudging 2,000 feet high. The glen did not have so much as a path through it and could be approached from the sea only by clambering up the rocks. Prince Charlie spent twenty-two idyllic days there, free from stress, yet within sight of Royal Navy ships patrolling the Minch.

A cave at Corodale is claimed by tradition to have been the Prince's refuge, but contemporary accounts describe his hiding place as a forester's hut, and certainly the comforts he enjoyed there suggest something more luxurious than a cave. Perhaps he did hide in a cave briefly while MacEachain checked out whether the hut was safe.

Peace of mind at Corodale was brittle; during much of the time his health, both mental and physical, was poor, and he continued to suffer from dysentery and mood swings which swept him from wild manic highs to deep depression. At times he would just sit silently for long periods. However, Clanranald friends turned the Corodale hut into a place far superior to anywhere he had hidden previously. A Clanranald officer, Captain Alexander MacDonald, recalled that the Prince had his own little moss-covered, earthen seat with a plaid laid over it for a throne, and here he held court for clansmen who trudged over the hills to visit him. Around him were O'Sullivan, MacEachain, Felix O'Neil, an assortment of MacDonalds and a dozen other 'sturdy clever fellows', who acted as guards and ran errands.

Life at Corodale was unharried by redcoats or militia and Charlie was able to spend his days hunting and fishing. He would clamber down the rocks to the seashore and fish with hand lines for lythe, a species of small cod, or he would hunt in the hills. Captain Alexander MacDonald recalled these shooting expeditions: 'His royal highness was pretty oft at his diversion through the mountain, papping down perhaps dozens in a day of muircocks and hens, with which this place abounds. For he is most dextrous at shooting all kinds of fowl upon the wing, scarce ever making a miss.' He could imitate the call of the plover so perfectly that the birds flew towards him, and he shot many of them – some Highlanders thought it was witchcraft.

One day the Prince shot a deer, which Ned Burke gralloched and butchered for their larder, but this animal almost cost Charles his freedom. A small boy in rags appeared at Ned's side while he was preparing the carcase, and reached out to touch the meat. Ned aimed a blow at the lad with the back of his hand, but the Prince scolded him. 'You ought rather to give him meat than a strip[e],' he said, and insisted that the boy be given some better clothes as well as a hunk of the venison. Several weeks later the boy betrayed Charles to the militia, but fortunately they did not believe him.

MacDonald friends, known to have visited Corodale regularly, included Boisdale and Hugh of Baleshare (captain of a militia company hunting the Prince!). There were other unnamed visitors as well, probably among them Hugh MacDonald of Armadale in Skye (another militia officer) and Angus MacDonald of Milton in South Uist, step-father and brother respectively of Flora MacDonald, who were soon to play an important part in the escape drama.

While the men hunted and drank with the fugitive, their wives contributed to his comfort: Lady Clanranald sent shirts and Lady Boisdale food and other clothing. Even the Sleat chief's wife Lady Margaret MacDonald, whose husband was safely away at Fort Augustus serving with Cumberland, managed to smuggle 50 guineas to him, as well as clothes and newspapers – delivered by one of her husband's militia officers. A uniform was no proof of which side a clansman served on, and as the hunt for the Prince intensified this became ever more apparent.

It has often been said that it was during this summer that Charles Stuart began the slide towards the alcoholism that destroyed him in later life. Certainly there must have been a temptation to drink brandy to keep out the cold and dampness, but his father had worried about his son's drinking even before he left Rome. By the time he reached Corodale the Prince had a good head for alcohol and usually offered his visitors neat brandy, which they drank from clean shells while he used his prized silver cup. One carousal became legendary, when he drank everybody under the table, including Boisdale, reputedly one of the hardest drinkers in the whole of Scotland. When it ended Charles reverentially covered the casualties with plaids and sang 'De Profundis' over them before leaving them to sleep it off. One remarked afterwards, 'Never have I seen a punch bowl attacked more freely or frankly.'

While Charles enjoyed himself at Corodale, the rape of the Highlands continued. During May and June the hunt for the Prince widened, with Cumberland moving his headquarters to Fort Augustus in the third week of May to bring him closer to West Highland Jacobite heartlands. The Campbell militia were also let loose in Morar and Moidart and, as Charles had discovered on his journey to Stornoway, Royal Navy patrols intensified among the islands.

In spite of all this effort the Prince and the majority of clan leaders escaped every trap; the chiefs who remained behind after the *Mars* and *Bellone* had returned to France held a council at which Lord Lovat was present and proposed a guerrilla campaign, for which he promised 400 Fraser clansmen. Suspicious of the old fox, Murray of Broughton drew up a bond of good faith, but Lovat refused to put his name to it. Nor did the promised Fraser men appear. Murray realised that he and Lochiel were virtually the only leaders still committed to the summer campaign, and both felt betrayed by fellow chiefs and the Prince.

There was a good deal of backbiting among the chiefs who stayed behind, with Lovat deeply immersed in yet more treachery, while Lochgarry and others were accused of thieving from other clans. Murray, still weak after the illness that struck before Culloden, complained bitterly that Aeneas MacDonald, the banker, was accusing him of mismanaging the Prince's money, and he now gave up and set out for the Continent. He was betrayed and captured on the way. Aeneas MacDonald surrendered to General Campbell, and, prize of prizes, Lord Lovat was captured on an island on Loch Morar, hiding in a hollow tree, they said. However, another version claimed he was found lying comfortably on the two feather beds that were required to hold his fat carcase – this has the ring of truth. Cumberland couldn't wait to inform the Duke of Northumberland in London about this success: 'I imagine that the taking of Lord Lovat is a greater Humiliation and vexation to the Highlanders than anything that could have happened, as he is dignified with great Titles, and ranks high in command,' he crowed. Title and rank were of no help to old Simon Fraser now. He was taken to London to be tried the following year and executed on Tower Hill on 9 April 1747. His life may have been treacherous, but Lovat died well: on the block he calmly handed his executioner a purse containing 10 guineas and told him, 'Pray do your work well, for if you should cut and hack my shoulders I shall be able to rise again. I shall be very angry.'

The Highlands were full of secrets and yet there remained few secrets there that summer. Cumberland kept losing the scent of his quarry, but picking it up again, and by the middle of June he learned from several sources that the Prince had not escaped in the *Mars* or *Bellone*, but was still in the Hebrides. The Presbyterian ministers of South Uist and Harris had passed the information to the MacLeod chief, and the man from whom they attempted to hire a boat at Stornoway had betrayed him, but so too had Aeneas MacDonald and Lord Lovat. The banker admitted that Charles had been at Stornoway, and Lovat actually revealed that he was at that moment hiding on Uist. It is easy to condemn prisoners, particularly men as slippery as Simon Fraser, for breaking down under interrogation, but it seems that MacDonald and Fraser talked just that bit too readily. MacDonald may have believed that he was revealing nothing more than they already knew, but when Lord Lovat talked about Uist he must have been aware that they would realise Charles was among friends on the island, and attention would turn to Clanranald and Boisdale – which is precisely what happened.

Nevertheless, some brave MacDonald clansmen were passing false information to the government at the same time, which persuaded General Campbell to rush off suddenly to Tobermory to search Mull and the southern islands of the Outer Hebrides, then to sail with several hundred men to St Kilda, that lonely scatter of islands more than 30 miles

Benbecula Causeway. The islands of North Uist, Benbecula and South Uist were separated by narrow straits that could be forded on foot at low tide. Today causeways carry a road all the way from Lochmaddy to Lochboisdale.

out in the Atlantic beyond the Long Island. Bewildered St Kildans were frightened out of their wits.

'The poor creatures were quite amazed,' Bishop Forbes was told, 'and declared they knew nothing of that man, for they had never heard of him before. They said they had heard a report that their Laird, MacLeod, had lately been at war with a great woman abroad, but that he had got the better of her, and that was all they knew of the disturbances in the world.' The islanders probably understood little of events of recent months, so it was a masterstroke of disinformation on the part of whoever sowed the St Kilda seeds in General Campbell's mind.

The St Kilda red herring cost the searchers valuable time, but provided the fugitive with no more than temporary respite. Cumberland's intelligence told him his quarry was still on the Long Island – almost certainly in the Uists – so the search was concentrated there. The MacLeod and MacDonald of Sleat militia were ordered to the Outer Isles, but the Sleat chief himself managed to remain well out of the hunt at Fort Augustus. Sir Alexander secretly admitted that he was frightened he might capture the Prince, and thus bring terrible shame on his clan.

Two great sweeps of the Long Island were begun simultaneously from the north and the south – a thorough and systematic combing of the Outer Hebrides from end to end, which was bound to penetrate sooner or later to Corodale. Boisdale hurried to warn Charles it was time to move on, and so, on 6 June, there began a renewed pursuit which pushed Prince Charlie from one adventure and narrow escape to another. It was a time of hardship that was to test the Prince's character as never before and

Old timbers of a boat that has made its last Hebridean journey.

stretch his physical powers to their limit. Fortunately, he was as fit as ever – probably fitter – so he could cope with physical pain. While crossing a burn on Uist he missed his step and fell on a pointed rock, injuring his ribs, but picked himself up with a heavy groan and walked on, grinding his teeth whenever the pain struck.

Donald MacLeod had returned from the mainland by now, and he sailed with the Prince from Corodale to the rugged little island of Wiay off the south-eastern tip of Benbecula, where Clanranald sent news. The seas around the island were being patrolled with increasing intensity and that a MacLeod militia company had actually landed on Wiay. Lieutenant William MacLeod, in charge of the search, either missed the fugitives or had Jacobite sympathies and turned a blind eye. For whatever reason Donald MacLeod who remained on the island was not discovered.

Charles had no choice but to return to Corodale, which was at least still safe: but with so many sea patrols that would not be easy. However, old Donald and O'Sullivan bravely sailed to Rossinish to pick up Charlie and O'Neil, then set out for Corodale under cover of darkness. Off the South Uist coast a violent storm blew up and they were forced to put into Usinish Point a mile or two short of their destination. The only shelter from the wind and rain was a cleft in the rocks at Acarseid Fhalaich, where they huddled for the remainder of the night and the whole of the next miserable day.

On the following day they sailed on to Kyle Stuley, where the Prince had the narrowest escape of the whole of his wanderings. His boat was nearly run down by the *Baltimore* and the *Raven* on one of their patrols, but the dark night enabled the fugitives to slip ashore unobserved and spend the remainder of the night in another rock cleft. In the morning they could no longer see the enemy ships, but on trying to enter Loch Eynort they found the *Baltimore* still there and had to creep back to their rock cleft and lie low all day with the warship less than 2 miles away. By next morning the *Baltimore* had gone.

On 15 June, thanks to Donald MacLeod's brilliant seamanship, they arrived safely at Loch Boisdale, having eluded the fleet of warships and small boats now crowding the Uist coast. Ned reported seeing no fewer than fifteen sails at one point, and on another occasion Donald thought he spotted sails of two French ships. Unfortunately, these turned out to be British men-of-war. It was a near miracle that they were able to reach an old tower (probably Calvay) at the mouth of the loch and conceal themselves there.

They remained at Loch Boisdale for almost a week, with the Prince taking to the mountains during the day and sleeping in open fields under boat sails on several nights, and moving swiftly and surreptitiously whenever a militia group was spotted. MacDonald of Boisdale, they discovered, had been arrested and taken aboard HMS *Furnace* for

On Sheaval hill. Here the Flora MacDonald legend began at the shieling on Flora's brother's summer pastures. Prince Charlie came to the heroine and she agreed to escort him over the sea to Skye disguised as her maid.

questioning by Captain Ferguson, and Neil MacEachain bravely made a night walk to Kilbride to talk to Lady Boisdale, who had also been held prisoner, but was now freed. He brought back food and comforts for the Prince, but also bad news about the hunt.

It had been hoped that the Prince might sail south to Barra, which had already been searched, but Lady Boisdale told Neil that one of the most notorious Hanoverian Army commanders, Captain Caroline Scott, had landed on the island of Flodday in the Sound of Barra and was expected on South Uist imminently. In fact he arrived at Kilbride on the morning of Sunday 22 June, but by that time Prince Charlie had vanished again – and his Clan Donald friends had yet another plan in hand.

Leaving all other members of the party to fend for themselves, Charles had set out the previous day with only O'Neil and MacEachain, as guide, to walk north, and seek shelter among the empty hills behind Ormiclett, formerly the home of the Clanranald chief but abandoned after it was destroyed during the '15 rising. It was midnight when MacEachain led them to a cave on Ben Ruigh Choinnich, and here they paused to discuss how Charles might be taken off the Long Island.

One of the Clanranald MacDonalds from the mainland said a committee meeting on a hilltop 'pitched upon the stratagem', but the plan has the hallmarks of a single man's inspiration, and he is one of the least talked about figures in the entire escape legend. Hugh MacDonald of Armadale in Skye had led an adventurous life which included service with the French Army during which he lost an eye and gained a nickname, Uisdean Cam ('One-eyed Hugh' in Gaelic). A less romantic tale suggested that he lost the eye when he was struck accidentally by a tree during his boyhood. Whichever may be the true version, Hugh returned from France and married Marion, widow of a member of a Uist branch of the clan – it is said that he swept her off her feet quite literally by carrying her away to Skye to marry him. By her first marriage Marion had had three children, of whom two survived: Angus, who farmed at Milton in South Uist, and Flora, who lived with her mother and step-father on Skye. In the '45 'One-eyed' Hugh served as a captain in MacDonald of Sleat's militia, but his sympathies, like those of his chief, inclined towards the Stuarts. In June 1746 Hugh was on Uist leading one of the militia companies now combing the islands for the Prince, and while no one admitted it in so many words, 'Uisdean Cam' was almost certainly the man behind the plot to spring Prince Charlie from Cumberland's trap.

The plan was that the Prince should be spirited off the island disguised as Hugh's step-daughter's maid. And at that very moment Flora was conveniently alone minding her brother's cattle at his shieling, or hut, at Alisary on the summer pastures on Sheaval hill, above Milton, and close to the hiding place on Ruigh Choinnich. Unless Flora's presence at Alisary was part of a carefully arranged plan, it seems inconceivable that a

22-year-old woman, even one as a capable as Flora MacDonald, would have been allowed to spend the night alone at a remote hut while the island was swarming with militiamen.

It is hard to establish whether Flora had been told in advance of the plan. Her kinsman MacEachain and O'Neil, who were probably jealous of one another, gave different versions of Flora's first meeting with the Prince, each claiming the honour of introducing her to Charles. Felix O'Neil wrote that he went to the hut and asked Flora about militia movements in the area and then told her he had brought a friend to see her. 'She with some emotion asked if it was the Prince,' he recounted. 'I answered in the affirmative and instantly brought him in.' MacEachain claimed it was he who woke Flora, but she had 'got scarcely on half of her close [clothes], when the prince, with his baggage upon his back was at the door, and saluted her very kindly.'

As for Flora, she contradicted herself. Soon after the event, when she may still have felt it necessary to protect MacEachain, she wrote, 'Captain O'Neil brought Miss MacDonald to the place where the Prince was.' Later she said Felix 'sent in a cousine of her own, who had been along with him and the Prince, to awake her.'

MacEachain's version sounds the more believable since he, as one of her own kinsmen, would be the man most likely to approach her in the middle of the night, and the bursting in of the stranger carrying a pack on his back bears all the hallmarks of the Prince. It took much coaxing before Flora agreed to the plan to escort Prince Charlie to Skye dressed as her maidservant, but, having made the decision, she set about carrying it out bravely. She left the following morning for Clanranald's house on Benbecula to make arrangements, with Charles waiting in the mountains close to Corodale.

Unfortunately, Flora's journey meant crossing from South Uist to Benbecula by the ford (there was no causeway in those days), and there she was detained by the militia because she had no permit to travel. The soldiers, who happened to be MacLeods, held her overnight, but fortunately her step-father, 'One-eyed' Hugh, arrived in the morning and ordered her to be set free. To Flora's horror, as she breakfasted with her step-father, Neil MacEachain, who was still supposed to be hiding with the Prince, was brought in. He too had been caught at the ford because Charles' impetuosity had nearly ruined another plan. The Prince had considered that Flora was taking too long to return, so had forced poor, weary Neil to set off in search of her and he was captured. Luckily, as 'One-eyed' Hugh was able to vouch for MacEachain, he and Flora were both freed.

Briefly, an alternative scheme was considered, to take the Prince to the isolated island of Fladda-Chuain off the northern point of Skye, but that was known to be well guarded. Charles' MacDonald friends reverted to the original idea of spiriting him across the Minch to Skye in disguise as Flora's

FLORA MACDONALD –
A LEGEND IN HER LIFETIME

lora MacDonald, heroine of Prince Charlie's escape, was just two years younger than the Prince, whom she escorted over the sea to Skye dressed as her maid Betty Burke. She was born in South Uist in 1722, the daughter of Ranald and Marion MacDonald, but her father died when she was still a baby, and when her mother remarried she moved to Armadale in Skye with her mother and step-father.

When Prince Charlie was trapped on South Uist she agreed to accompany him to Skye, and on the night of 28 June she and the Prince made the legendary voyage – to freedom for the Prince and to gaol for Flora. Eventually, she was taken to London, where she was held prisoner for a year, although she was never brought to trial.

After her return to Skye she married Allan MacDonald of Kingsburgh, but

*Flora MacDonald
by Allan Ramsay, 1749.*

The statue to the heroine in Inverness.

unfortunately Allan was not a good manager of money and they soon found themselves in financial difficulties. They emigrated to North Carolina in 1774 and settled at Cheeks Creek in Anson County (later Mongomery County) just as the War of Independence broke out. Allan joined the loyalists, thus Flora MacDonald found herself on the losing side again. Allan was captured and taken to Philadelphia, leaving Flora in Carolina, where she suffered much hardship and lost many of her possessions.

The cairn marking Flora MacDonald's birthplace in South Uist.

When Allan was freed they were reunited in New York and then moved to Nova Scotia, intending to settle there, but after one bitter winter they returned to Skye. Flora died in 1790 and her husband two years later. She is buried at Kilmuir on Skye.

Dr Samuel Johnson, who met her in 1773 during his tour of the Hebrides, wrote Flora's epitaph: 'Her name will be mentioned in history, and if courage and fidelity be virtues, mentioned with honour.'

Flora meeting Dr Johnson at Kingsburgh during his visit to Skye in 1773.

Background: *Benbecula Causeway.*

Irish maidservant Betty Burke, and then back to the mainland. Why the name Betty Burke? Betty was a common enough first name, and since the girl was supposed to be Irish (to cover the Prince's slightly foreign accent) what better surname than Burke after the loyal Ned Burke?

Flora, Lady Clanranald and other women at the Clanranald chief's house then began to sew furiously to make a quilted petticoat, a gown of patterned calico and a white apron over which Charles was to wear a dun cloak with a large hood 'after the Irish fashion'. A cap designed to hide as much of his face as possible completed the Betty Burke disguise.

On the night of 23 June MacEachain took Charles back to Wiay, and on the following day to Rossinish: the barren rocks of these parts of the Long Island were all becoming familiar to Prince Charlie, and so was the weather – as miserable as on his past visits. On the 25th they had to flee into open country when militiamen turned up unexpectedly, and spent the entire day in the open air, sheltering under a rock in pouring rain.

By the morning of Friday 27 June everything was ready and two young MacDonald officers of the militia arrived to tell the Prince they would sail that night. Flora, her brother Angus, Lady Clanranald and Lady Clan's young daughter Margaret arrived from Nunton, and Charles tried on his Betty Burke costume to the amusement of everybody present. Charles did not mind Lady Clanranald laughing at the 'jocose drollery' of this dress rehearsal for his role as Betty Burke, for he was already an expert in disguise and aliases and remained so all his life. Just before the '45, while the French were planning their unsuccessful invasion of England, he revelled in living unrecognised at Gravelines, and told his father in a letter dated 15 April 1744: 'Everyone is wondering where the Prince is, and sometimes he is told news of himself to his face, which is very diverting.' And later, when his Cause was lost Charles wandered from country to country as the wild man of Europe, using a variety of disguises and aliases. Charles took easily to his role as Betty Burke, but did not forget his rank.

When Charles was dressed the household sat down to a meal, at which he took care to show princely courtliness towards the ladies, setting Flora on his right hand and Lady Clanranald on his left. There was much conversation and laughter as the meal began, yet the Prince could not hide his nervousness as he veered from deep thoughtfulness to nervous high spirits, until a messenger arrived with news that General Campbell himself had landed near Clanranald's house with 1,500 men. The merrymaking turned to panic, which MacEachain described vividly: 'All run to their boat in the greatest confusion, every one carrying with him whatever part of the baggage came first to his hand, without either regard to sex or quality, they crossed to Lochisguiway [Loch Uiskevagh], and about five in the morning, landed on the other side, where they had supper.'

While those who had any appetite left by then ate, news reached them that not only was Campbell accompanied by the feared Captain Ferguson but they had actually arrived at Clanranald's house and Ferguson had the audacity to sleep in Lady Clan's bed. Caroline Scott was on his way too, having scoured South Uist without success. The net was that near to closing on the Prince. O'Neil estimated that about 2,000 government soldiers must be on Benbecula at that moment for the final sweep. Campbell was either very fortunate or singularly well informed to arrive at this juncture – probably just lucky – and could easily have taken the Prince that night but for the MacDonalds.

As Lady Clan hurried home, 'One-eyed' Hugh sent Flora a letter to guarantee his step-daughter safe conduct in case she should be stopped by the military, and final preparations were made for departure. Charles insisted on keeping his pistols under his petticoat, but Flora would have none of it. If they were searched, the firearms would give him away, she told him. 'Indeed, Miss,' Charles answered, 'if we shall happen to meet with any that will go so narrowly to work in searching as what you mean, they will certainly discover me at any rate.' Her brother took the pistols and passed them to 'One-eyed' Hugh. She did allow him to keep his 'crab stick', a short heavy cudgel, which he carried everywhere to fend off attack.

At about eight o'clock on the evening of Saturday, 28 June, Flora, her 'maid' Betty Burke and Neil MacEachain set out on the journey that was to become the lynchpin of the Prince Charlie legend – the voyage over the sea to Skye. The small boat was crewed by Lieutenants John and Roderick MacDonald, Ensign Roderick MacDonald – on unofficial 'leave' from their militia companies – Duncan Campbell and John MacMhuirich.

It was a clear evening when they set sail into the gathering darkness, so they had to watch carefully for enemy ships as they nosed among the skerries into open sea. With hardly a breath of wind they made slow progress at the start, but soon a real Hebridean squall blew up, as fierce and unexpected as storms can strike in those parts. Soon the gale was whipping up rough, tempestuous seas and rain poured down. With neither shelter nor comfort the Prince, a seasoned Hebridean sailor by now – or perhaps so relieved to be out of the trap, kept their spirits up by singing the Jacobite songs, 'The 29th of May' and 'The King Shall Enjoy his Own Again'.

Flora recounted afterwards that she fell asleep during the night and woke suddenly to find the Prince leaning over her with his hands over her face. He explained that the crewmen had to adjust the sail and he feared that in the dark they might trample on her. How Flora's admirers loved this story in years to come.

By morning the wind had died away and a mist crept over the sea, so that the boatmen had to lower their sail and row gently, stopping often to listen for the sound of the sea breaking on the rocky shore, which they knew must be close. As they drifted in the eddying currents a wind rose again without warning and drove the mist off to reveal cliffs. They were at Waternish Point,

From Skye sunset lights up the Hebrides and the sea over which Prince Charlie made the voyage dressed as Flora's Irish maid Betty Burke.

and on the sabbath morning there was not a soul to be seen. But as they approached the oarsmen suddenly realised they were mistaken – this was not Waternish at all, but Dunvegan Head, well to the south and west of Waternish. And it lay in not-to-be-trusted MacLeod territory.

They grabbed their oars and rowed fiercely against a strengthening north-westerly until they rounded the point, and saw ahead the stark, but welcome, black basalt face of Waternish. By now the men were so exhausted and making such desperately slow progress in spite of all their efforts that the Prince volunteered to take a turn at the oars. His help was refused. They could not allow the heir to the royal house to row them like a common boatman. Wearily they rowed the small craft round Waternish until they reached Ardmore, a little bay on the west side, where the vessel could be beached safely.

As they neared the shore a voice from the beach called to them to land, and to their horror they saw two militiamen with a small boat beached close to the place where they had intended to go ashore. Nearby stood a hut where the remainder of their company were no doubt enjoying a sabbath-morning rest, which would soon be disturbed. One of the men aimed his musket and fired, but missed, and the fugitives gave him no time to reload. Finding strength from heaven alone knew where, the crew took up their oars and began to row out to sea for dear life.

'The poor men, almost ready to breathe out their last, at length made the point of Watersay,' Neil MacEachain recalled, but by the time they had rounded the point out of sight they could go no further, so they manoeuvred the little craft into a deep cleft in the rocks. They were given some bread and butter and fresh water from one of the little waterfalls that tumble down Waternish cliff face, then rested for an hour until they felt sure they had not been pursued.

Taking advantage of the cover the scattered Ascrib islands offered, they rowed across the broad mouth of Loch Snizort towards the Trotternish peninsula, and beached their boat at a small bay close to Totescore a little north of Uig – at a place still called Prince Charlie's Point. It was two o'clock on Sunday afternoon, and they were 'within cannon shot' of Sleat chief Sir Alexander MacDonald's home, which lay conveniently out of sight just over a low hill. Prince Charlie had been carried safely over the sea to Skye.

A rainbow marks the end of a shower at Prince Charlie's Point, near Uig, where the Prince landed at the end of the journey to Skye.

'THE DEVIL CANNOT FIND US NOW'

Leaving Prince Charlie on the shore in the care of the boatmen, Flora and Neil MacEachain hurried to Monkstadt, where their arrival destroyed the deep sabbath-day calm. Sir Alexander had left only the day before to join Cumberland at Fort Augustus, and Lady Margaret was just sitting down to dinner with three guests, Mrs MacDonald of Kirkibost, who had arrived from the Long Island the previous day, the Sleat factor (land steward) Alexander MacDonald of Kingsburgh and Lieutenant Alexander MacLeod, 'a sneaking little

The sharp-toothed rock pillars of the Quiraing stand sheer against the north Skye skyline.

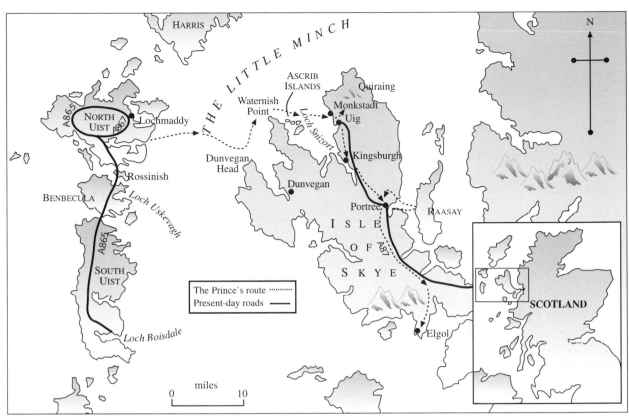

28 June–4 July. Over the sea to Skye, then through Skye to Raasay and on to Elgol.

gentleman' in charge of the militia guarding this part of the coast – commander of the men who had chased Prince Charlie's boat at Ardmore.

Flora quietly passed a message to Lady Margaret, who must have known that the Prince was on his way but not when, and she panicked now because of the militia officer's presence in the house. Should Charles Stuart be arrested here she and her husband would surely be accused of aiding him – quite justifiably in view of the fact that Sleat's militiamen had helped to organise the Betty Burke scheme, and Lady Margaret had been in touch with the Prince and sent him presents at Corodale. Her ladyship rushed around madly, demanding that Donald Roy MacDonald of Baleshare be sent for, further proof of her involvement since Baleshare had charge of the Skye end of the escape plot.

Flora prevailed on her to find some excuse to bring Kingsburgh from the dinner table, while she would keep Lieutenant MacLeod engaged in conversation. Kirkibost's wife, who knew nothing of the Prince's arrival, delivered a note to summon Donald Roy, and while Lady Margaret, Kingsburgh and Donald Roy paced up and down the garden debating the next move, Flora sat with the lieutenant, calmly discussing rumours of the Prince's presence that were circulating on the Long Island. This ability to

Prince Charles Edward Stuart as Betty Burke by J. Williams.

remain composed and tell a plausible story was to stand Flora in good stead in the weeks to come.

Neil returned to the boat and brought Prince Charlie to a safe place near Monkstadt. As they walked, Neil suggested Charles should carry a bundle of light clothing to add authenticity to the Betty Burke disguise, but before they had gone far the Prince threw the bundle down and told Neil petulantly to carry it himself or leave it there. Betty Burke was behaving true to the 'lazy jade' character everyone had been told to give her – and faithfully to the Stuart Prince's sense of his own royalty.

Another incident soon followed when Charles remembered that he had left his case of knives behind. Had Neil brought them from the boat? No. Then he must go back for them. Neil protested that it was unsafe to leave the Prince there in the open, but Charles would have none of it. 'Do you what you are ordered,' he snapped, 'for I must absolutely have it, so no more words.' Neil obediently returned to the boat, and when Kingsburgh arrived with some food a little later he found the fugitive easily. Instead of lying low, the restless Charlie was wandering about and had disturbed a flock of sheep.

Towards nightfall the factor set out to lead him and MacEachain to his own house at Kingsburgh, on the shores of Loch Snizort a few miles south of Uig. Flora told the lieutenant that in these unsettled times she was anxious to be on her way home to Armadale, and left too, accompanied by Mrs MacDonald of Kirkibost and Mrs MacDonald's maid. They did not actually accompany the Prince, but remained close enough to note the alarm he was causing to his companions by taking long unwomanly strides and holding his petticoats indecently high at a ford. Homegoing churchgoers were muttering so much about this odd behaviour that Neil at one point cried out, 'For God's sake, Sir, take care what you are doing.' But Charles just laughed.

Mrs MacDonald and her maid kept staring at Betty Burke too, until the maid was driven to declare Flora's maid the most impudent-looking woman she had ever seen and that she must either be an Irishwoman or man in woman's dress. Flora assured them her maid was an Irishwoman, and hurried them on.

It was about midnight before they reached the factor's house, wet and miserable, and there they found everybody had gone to bed – Kingsburgh's wife Florence, his daughter Anne and Anne's husband Ranald MacAlister of Skirinish, who was an officer in the militia. Kingsburgh sent a maid to tell his wife that the master had arrived home with company. Mrs MacDonald was not pleased to be disturbed. 'What company?' she asked.

'Milton's daughter, I believe, and some company with her,' the girl replied.

The mistress had no intention of rising to entertain Flora MacDonald or anyone else at that time of night. 'Milton's daughter is very welcome to

All that remains of Monkstadt, home of Sir Alexander MacDonald of Sleat.

Kingsburgh, south of Uig, was the home of the Sleat chief's factor Alexander MacDonald. The house was altered considerably after the Prince's visit, but is now a ruin.

come here with any company she pleases to bring. But you'll give my service to her and tell her to make free with anything in the house for I am very sleepy and cannot see her this night.'

At that moment Anne rushed into her mother's bedroom in a great state of agitation. 'O mother,' she wailed, 'my father has brought in a very odd, muckle, ill-shapen-up wife as ever I saw, and he has gone into the hall with her.' While Florence was searching her mind to fathom why her husband should bring some strange-looking woman into the best room in the house, Kingsburgh himself appeared and ordered her 'to fasten on her bucklings again' and get some supper for him and his visitors.

'Pray, good man, what company is this you have brought with you?' she demanded.

'You shall know that in due time,' was all he would tell her, and Anne was sent to fetch her mother's keys from the hall, but returned, too terrified to enter the room because there was 'a muckle woman' walking up and down in the room. Mrs MacDonald steeled herself to collect the keys herself, but as soon as she entered the room the stranger approached and took her hand and kissed it. She froze as the bristles of the stranger's beard made her realise that this was some poor Jacobite fugitive. But she still had no idea it was the Prince.

She returned to her husband who told her she had just met Prince Charles Edward Stuart. Her first reaction was fear. 'We will a' be hanged now,' she wailed, but he just told her cheerfully, 'We will die but once; and if we are hanged for this, I am sure we die in a good cause. Pray, make no delay; go, get some supper.'

Next Florence complained in true housewifely fashion that she had no food suitable for a royal guest, but Kingsburgh ordered her simply to make what she had to hand without fuss lest she alert the servants. According to her husband, she produced 'roasted eggs, collops [slices of meat], plenty bread and butter', and the Prince insisted that she should sit beside him at the table. Both Kingsburgh and his wife said the Prince looked well; his face was sunburned, but apart from some raw patches on his legs, caused by wearing wet stockings, he had not an itch on his body as his enemies claimed – they had put rumours about that he was 'scabbed to the eye-holes'.

When the meal was finished Charles drank a toast to his host and hostess, and the women retired, leaving Kingsburgh, Neil MacEachain and the Prince to drink punch well into the night. Charles produced an old broken pipe bound together with thread and explained that he had begun to smoke during his time in hiding. Kingsburgh brought out a brand new

Portree harbour. Portree, whose name in Gaelic means the King's Port, was named in honour of a royal visit by Charles' ancestor James V. The Prince's stay there was no royal progress however – he spent only a few hours in an inn on the site of the present-day Royal Hotel.

Portree looking towards
Nicolson's Rock, where Charles
landed on his return from
Raasay.

pipe and tobacco, and Charles smoked contentedly while he talked. Eventually, he washed and retired to bed between clean sheets for the first time since Culloden. No mention is made of Anne's husband, the militia lieutenant, in all this, and one can only assume that he tactfully slipped away so that he could never be accused of being party to the treasonable offence of giving support to Charles Stuart.

In the morning Mrs MacDonald went to Flora's bedroom and demanded to hear every detail of the journey from Uist, and when Flora had finished the factor's wife asked what had happened to the boat and crew. She was horrified to learn that they had returned to South Uist. Florence MacDonald was a wise woman for she told Flora, 'I wish you had sunk the boat and kept the boatmen in Skye where they could have been concealed . . . because his enemies by this means would have lost scent of him'.

The thought had not occurred to Flora, so she now rushed to Kingsburgh and begged him to wake the Prince and get him on his way.

However, the factor found the Prince still in such a sound sleep that he did not have the heart to rouse him. That night Prince Charlie slept for nine or ten hours, probably longer than any night since he had left Rome.

When he awoke, Mrs MacDonald forced Flora to go and ask for a lock of hair as a keepsake. Bishop Forbes described the incident:

> Mrs MacDonald, taking hold of Miss with one hand, knocked at the door of the room with the other. The Prince called, 'Who is there?' Mrs MacDonald, opening the door, said 'Sir, it is I, and I am importuning Miss Flora to come in and get a lock of your hair to me, and she refuses to do it.' 'Pray,' said the Prince, 'desire Miss MacDonald to come in. What should make her afraid to come where I am?' When Miss came in he begged her to sit down on a chair at the bedside, then laying his arms about her waist, and his head upon her lap, he desired her to cut out the lock with her own hands in token of future and more substantial favours. One half of the lock Miss gave to Mrs MacDonald and the other she kept to herself.

It was late afternoon before Charles was ready to leave, dressed once more in his Betty Burke costume in case one of the Kingsburgh servants should be alerted, but he carried one of Ranald MacAlister's kilts to change into when he was clear of the house. He was accompanied by Neil MacEachain and a young lad named MacQueen as guide, and Kingsburgh walked with them as far as the wood where the Prince changed into MacAlister's outfit. With a claymore in his hand Prince Charlie was pronounced 'a soger-like man indeed' by the Sleat factor.

The parting was all the more heart-rending because the Prince suffered a slight nose bleed as he was saying goodbye to Kingsburgh: characteristically he dismissed it as something that only happened when he parted with a dear friend. Charles obviously thought he was saying farewell to Clan Donald country for he told the factor, 'Alas, Kingsburgh, I am afraid I shall not meet with another MacDonald in my difficulties.' He was wrong: the great clan still had a part to play in his escape and rescue.

The Betty Burke costume was hidden in a bush, but was retrieved afterwards, Mrs MacDonald converting the dress into a bed cover and giving the apron and Betty's blue velvet French garters to Flora. Most of the other garments were destroyed. The sheets the Prince had slept in were carefully folded away unwashed, and Mrs MacDonald asked her daughter to see that she was buried in one of them. The second was given to Flora, who also asked that it should be used as her shroud.

In darkness and unrelenting rain Charles was led across the muddy narrow hill track to Portree, where arrangements had been made for him

THE DEVIL CANNOT FIND US NOW'

to cross to the neighbouring island of Raasay, which had been searched already. Portree, in Gaelic 'Port an Righ' – Port of the King, was named after a visit by one of Charlie's ancestors, James V, in 1540, and although the principal centre of population on the island – as it still is – it comprised no more than a huddle of small thatched houses in 1746. MacQueen brought the Prince to Charles MacNab's inn, where Donald Roy was waiting with Flora, who had ridden by a shorter route and arrived ahead of him.

It was raining harder than ever and rain streamed off Charles' clothes, but when Donald Roy sympathised, he said he was more sorry for 'our Lady', as he usually called Flora. He was wet, weary, ravenous and badly in need of a dram, which was no problem since whisky was the one drink MacNab's house could offer. Prince Charlie stripped off everything except his wet shirt and wrapped his plaid around himself, then began to attack the landlord's fish and some cold chicken Kingsburgh had given him.

Watching Charles eating greedily, dressed only in a shirt, Donald Roy teased him: 'I believe that is the English fashion.'

'What fashion do you mean?' Charles asked.

'They say the English when they eat heartily, throw off their clothes.'

The Prince hardly paused. 'They are in the right lest anything should incommode their hands when they are at work,' he answered, and continued to eat contentedly. When his companions produced dry clothes he hesitated to put them on immediately: some thought this was because Flora was present, but the reason was much more likely to be that a prince of the royal blood could not be seen to dress in public. Donald Roy told him this was no time to stand on ceremony, so he began to dress himself in his fresh clothes without interrupting his meal while he did so.

When the Prince asked for something to drink with his meal he was told there was no beer or ale in the inn, which was only a whisky house, nor was there milk; he would have to drink water, which was kept in the bowl the landlord used to bail out his boat. When Donald Roy passed 'the ugly cog [bowl]', Charles eyed it suspiciously – the rim was bashed in with use and it looked none too clean. As the landlord was present Donald Roy whispered that the dish was clean enough and he should drink from it to avoid arousing suspicion. 'You are right,' said Charles and took a long draught.

The Prince had no intention of going out into the torrent of rain again that night, but Donald Roy insisted it was unsafe to remain on the island; he must leave with the MacLeods of Raasay who would take care of him. Charles begged Donald to come with them because he wanted at least one MacDonald at his side, but Donald assured him the Raasay clansmen would guard him. At the same time he put in a good word for the Sleat chief. 'Although Sir Alexander and his following did not join your royal highness, yet you see you have been very safe amongst them,' he told the

Overleaf: A fiery sunset over Raasay, where Charles spent only one night as the island had already been devastated by government troops, who returned only days later to lay it waste again.

Prince, 'for though they did not repair to your standard they wish you very well.' And he promised that if money were needed, Lady Margaret would provide him with all he required.

Resigned to having no choice but to part with the MacDonalds, the Prince bought some tobacco from the landlord, and in the early hours of Tuesday 1 July said his farewells to Neil and Flora. First he had to settle his financial debt to her: 'I believe, Madam, I owe you a crown of borrowed money,' he said. She assured him it was only half a crown, which he paid. He then kissed her hand and told her, 'For all that has happened I hope, Madam, we shall meet in St James' yet.' Flora MacDonald was never to see Prince Charlie again, in London or anywhere else, but she was never to forget him. How could she? The eleven days she had spent as his constant guardian overturned her life and made her a heroine.

One last effort to persuade Donald Roy to remain with him failed, but Donald did promise to rejoin him a couple of days later after he had reported to Lady Margaret and Kingsburgh. Flora stayed overnight at Portree and next morning MacEachain escorted her south to Armadale, where she explained to her mother that she had returned home because of 'things being in a hurry and confusion in South Uist, with such a number of military folks, she was uneasy till she got out of it'.

Donald walked back to Kingsburgh, then to Monkstadt, where Lady Margaret invited him to stay overnight. He accepted gladly because Lieutentant MacLeod of the militia was there again, and this gave him an opportunity to question MacLeod and his men casually about the Prince's movements. Donald Roy slept at MacLeod's headquarters, actually sharing the lieutenant's bed, and he had a long talk with the sentries guarding the coast. He was able to return to Portree confident that the hunters had no knowledge of the Prince's departure from the Long Island.

In the meantime, Charles arrived in Raasay, accompanied by two of the Laird of Raasay's sons, Murdoch and Malcolm MacLeod, and a cousin, Captain Malcolm MacLeod, and there he sheltered in a hut at Glam just across the Sound of Raasay from Skye. While Skye had been spared, Raasay had been ravaged because its chief had fought for the Prince. One of Captain Ferguson's officers had authorised the devastation of every house on the island and the killing of every animal they could find. They did a thorough job, and when the Prince arrived six weeks later an air of sullen emptiness still hung over the island.

The MacLeods looked after him well, but in this miserable hut at Glam Charles could not feel safe. Each time he looked across the narrow sound towards the mountains of Skye he was reminded that this low, bare, burnt island could offer him no safety should the vandals return. The sight of Portree reminded him of the Clan Donald friends he had left there, and that Donald Roy would be waiting. He made up his mind that he must return to Skye.

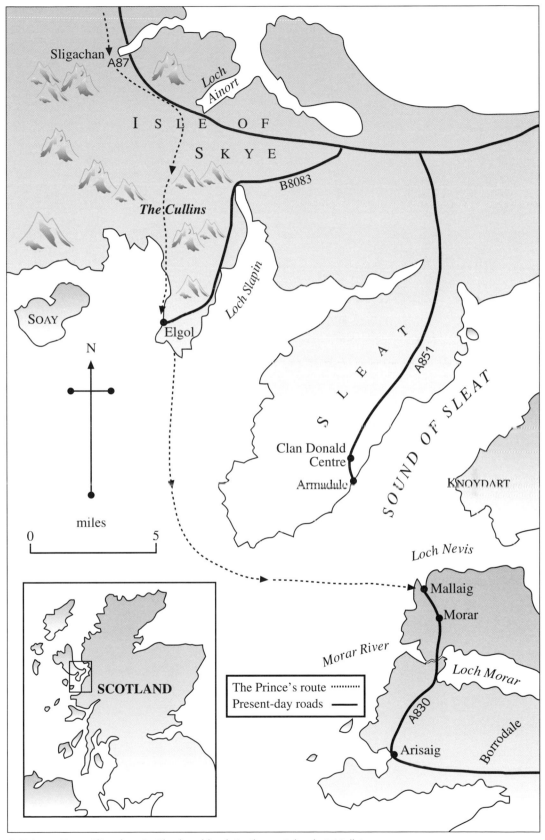

3–7 June. From Sligachan to Elgol and back to the mainland at Mallaig.

Coire Lagan in the Cuillins, typical of the wild bare mountains among which the Prince trekked on his journey through Skye.

Sligachan, where Charles and his guide had to make a detour to avoid a militia garrison stationed there as they walked through the Cuillins to the south of the island.

Charles' fears about the safety of Raasay were proved well grounded only days later when another pack of hunters descended upon the neighbouring small island of Rona and then Raasay itself, rounding up every man, woman and child and destroying the few animals or belongings they had missed in the earlier raid. They raped a blind girl and several other women, and flogged some of the men so cruelly that one of them never recovered from his injuries. For a further two months parties based on Skye continued to make raids on the island almost daily. Charles' companions were as much on edge as he was himself. When an itinerant packman appeared near their hut selling tobacco, they suspected him of being a spy and wanted to shoot him. Charles forbade that: better to leave the island, he said, than murder a man who might be innocent. On 2 July in yet another storm his MacLeod guardians rowed him back to Skye after only a couple of days on the island.

Nicolson's Rock, on the north side of Portree harbour, is pointed out as the Prince's landing place on his return, and his custodians said he slept in a cow byre that night. There is also a cave 4 miles north of Portree known as Prince Charles' Cave, although it is more likely that the landing place was Lag na Bachagh (the Hollow of the Byre) at Scorobreck, midway between Portree and the cave. Here, the Prince helped to haul the boat ashore, still wearing the very long, rain-soaked coat he had on during the voyage, then ate some crumbled oatcakes and cheese, the only food they had. After sending Young Raasay in search of Donald Roy, Charles lay down in his wet clothes and fell into a disturbed sleep, during which he started up every now and then, crying out, 'O poor England! O poor England!'

Having arranged to meet again at Camastianavaig, Murdoch MacLeod and the boatmen departed, leaving Captain Malcolm MacLeod, who had served with the Jacobite Army, alone with Charles in the cow byre. By evening the Prince's impatience got the better of him once more: having given up hope of Donald Roy returning, he suddenly asked Captain Malcolm whether he was a good walker and if he could walk bare-footed, meaning was he able to walk wearing only shoes without stockings as Charles used to do in Italy. The Captain had never gone 'bare-footed', but was willing to try, and in the byre the two prepared for the long trek through the Cuillins to the south-west corner of the island, which belonged to the MacKinnons, a clan every bit as loyal as the MacDonalds, although they have earned less glory in the escape story.

Charles took on a newfound authority that he had not displayed since before Culloden, but this was short-lived. At about six or seven in the evening he picked up his baggage, ordered the Captain to follow him and marched out across the moor, refusing to allow MacLeod to carry the baggage – a changed Charlie from the arrogance he had shown as Betty Burke. MacLeod followed obediently until the Prince took a direction that might lead towards a militia post and the Captain tactfully suggested that this way might be unwise. Charles then reverted to being the lost fugitive, utterly dependent on his clansman guide: 'Why, MacLeod, I now throw myself entirely into your hands, and leave you to do as you please,' he said with resignation. '. . . I hope you will accompany me, and you think you can can lead me safe enough into Strath'.

The Captain assured him he could, but would prefer to make the journey by sea; the overland journey meant nearly 30 long miles in the

A waterfall at Luib. With so much rain during the summer of 1746 every waterfall, including this one at Luib, was in full flow, making cross-country travel difficult.

In contrast to the wild splendour of the Cuillins, Loch Harport in MacLeod country is calm. The view looks toward Bracadale and Dunvegan.

Cuillins over byways and tracks on which they might well become lost in the darkness. But Charles would have none of this – he had seen enough of boats and storms around the islands, and was well accustomed to walking hill paths by night. He insisted they should set out on foot towards the Cuillins immediately.

Charles was still to travel as a servant, but this time as Lewie Caw, the son of a Crieff surgeon, who had actually been out in the campaign and was at that moment known to be skulking in Skye, and he carried off the role of male servant much better than that of a female. He was careful to walk behind his 'master' and insisted on carrying the baggage, and when MacLeod stopped to talk to anyone he sat down at a distance and waited.

From the byre at Scorobreck they had to make a detour westward to avoid Portree, then turn southwards along the lochside into Glen Varragill towards Sligachan, where another detour avoided the militia garrison. At Loch Ainort they followed the loch until they reached Strath Mor, where they turned south again to Loch Slapin and on past Kirkibost, home of the woman who had been at Monkstadt when Charles landed, to Elgol, where Captain MacLeod's sister lived.

Their route took them along muddy tracks beside lochs, over marshy, water-filled country and across high mountain ridges, and Charles coped with it all – even when he fell into a bog almost up to the top of his thighs and had to be pulled out by his armpits. It all seemed to exhilarate the Prince, who remained as fit as ever in spite of all the hardship he had undergone. The only problem on the long walk came when MacLeod noticed his companion fidgeting so uncomfortably he took him behind a small knowe and opened his shirt to find his body covered in lice, picked up no doubt in the cow byre or hut on Raasay. He now had the itch he talked of earlier and the Captain said he picked more than four score of lice from Charles' body.

The Prince drank a great deal of water while he walked and would stoop down and drink from a stream when he was warm and sweating, to the alarm of the Captain who thought cold water was bad for the hot body. MacLeod always offered him a dram immediately afterwards to counter the cold liquid, but Charles just laughed. 'No, no,' he protested, 'that will never hurt me in the least. If you happen to drink any cold thing when you are warm, only remember, MacLeod, to piss after drinking, and it will do you no harm at all. This advice I had from a friend abroad.' MacLeod noticed he was careful to heed his own advice. When their brandy bottle ran low and MacLeod tried to insist on the Prince having the last dram from it, Charles refused. MacLeod stood his ground until the Prince brought the great argument that ensued to an end by commanding the Captain to drink it. The clansman did, and then cannily hid the bottle in the bushes so that he might recover it sometime in the future and use it

Marsco peak. Beyond Sligachan the Prince struck into the Cuillins, following the valley of the River Sligachan but always hemmed in by Marsco and other dark peaks of the range.

again – and who knows, he told Charlie, this bottle might 'make a figure in Westminster yet'. MacLeod's bottle never reached London, but the Prince's greatcoat did – on the back of his MacLeod companion to whom he gave it before they parted.

As they walked the two men conversed on many matters, their talk inevitably turning to the rising. The Captain told Charles of the barbarities committed after Culloden, which shocked him greatly since he had seen no more of Cumberland's vengeance than what he had glimpsed on Raasay. He was bereft of words. 'Surely that man who calls himself the Duke, and pretends to be so great a general, cannot be guilty of such cruelties. I cannot believe them,' was all he could say. Then the conversation turned to Lord George Murray, whose conduct still rankled. Whether out of ignorance or betrayal, Charles said he did not know, but the Lieutenant-General would never obey his orders, especially during the days prior to Culloden when he 'did scarce one thing' he was asked to. Charles Stuart still did not understand the character of his best leader any more than Murray understood the Prince's.

Early in the morning of 4 July they reached Strath, where extra care was needed since many MacKinnons had been out in the rising. Charles, always fond of disguise, suggested he should blacken his face, but the Captain did not care for that. Instead the Prince pulled off his periwig, stuffed it into his pocket and took out a dirty white napkin which he tied on his head, then placed his hat on top. By this time he had had enough of this game. 'I think I will now pass well enough for your servant, and that I am sick with the much fatigue I have undergone. Look at me, MacLeod, and tell me what you think. How will it do?'

MacLeod was unhappy with this poor disguise, and was soon proved right for they encountered some men who had been in the Jacobite Army, and they recognised the fugitive at once. Charles was upset. 'This is an odd remarkable face I have got that nothing can disguise,' he moaned, but MacLeod believed it was not the Prince's face that was the problem, but the noble royal demeanour that was 'not ordinary'.

At Strath MacLeod's brother-in-law John MacKinnon looked after the fugitive well, and immediately set about making arrangements for him to be taken back to the mainland – and not a minute too soon.

During that first week of July when Charles was in the care of the Raasay MacLeods and the MacKinnons much happened to mislead Cumberland's forces and help the Prince. The Royal Navy wasted days chasing a French ship, *Le Hardi Mendiant*, which was sailing among the Hebridean isles in a desperate search for the Prince. She had succeeded in making contact with O'Sullivan who had fallen in with Felix O'Neil by chance and learned that the Prince was on Skye. O'Neil agreed to go to Skye to bring Charles to Lochmaddy, where the *Hardi Mendiant* would rendezvous with him. Felix had no luck in picking up the Prince's scent, which was as well because when he arrived back on Uist he discovered that the Frenchman had sailed.

Flora, normally so calm and composed, was furious and blamed this on O'Sullivan's cowardice. She told Bishop Forbes later 'the timorous Sullivan, having a fair wind, and not having courage to stay until O'Neil's return, being resolved to take care of Number One, obliged the captain to set sail directly, lest he should be taken and should lose his precious life.' Her verdict was harsh, for the French ship was being hunted by the Royal Navy and had been obliged to flee into the Atlantic. The chances of picking up the Prince were slim.

In spite of the *Hardi Mendiant* diversion, however, within ten days of Prince Charlie's arrival on Skye General Campbell had all the information he needed to pick up his quarry's trail again. Mrs MacDonald of Kingsburgh's worst fears came to pass: it had been a mistake to send the boatmen back to the Long Island. They were taken the moment they landed in Uist and Lachlan MacMhuirich confessed under threat of torture. As a result Clanranald and his wife were arrested; so too were the old boatman Donald MacDonald of Gualtergill and Felix O'Neil, who was taken at Rossinish after his return to Lochmaddy.

Campbell now knew every detail of the voyage over the sea to Skye: he had been told all about Betty Burke down to the last sprig of lilac pattern on the Irish maid's dress and he was fully apprised of the part Flora MacDonald and Kingsburgh played in the escape. He now felt confident enough to sail to Skye, where his first call was at the Sleat chief's house to interview Lady Margaret.

'Lady Margaret was surprised when she knew of our errand, told us most frankly upon our inquiry that Miss MacDonald had dined at her house on Sunday the 29th, that though she pressed her to stay all night, yet she could not prevail and that she had a man, and a maidservant with her. I think her ladyship did not know the maid's quality,' Campbell said of the interview. Her ladyship proved a very plausible liar, unless the general was tactfully trying to avoid the embarrassment of having to arrest the wife of a very important chief who was actually out fighting for King George. The latter seems the more likely explanation, but in any case Lady Margaret was only a bit player in the drama. There were other more guilty people to be questioned.

From Monkstadt Campbell and Captain Ferguson moved on to Kingsburgh, where Ferguson cunningly had one of the dairymaids brought on board the *Furnace* and questioned before he went to the factor's house. The girl told him everything she knew, even about the lock of hair the Prince had given her mistress. Armed with this information, the Captain of HMS *Furnace* went ashore and cross-examined Kingsburgh and his wife about Flora's visit, then asked in which room 'the person along with her in woman's clothes' slept. 'I know in what room

Blaven and the peaks of the Cuillins stood high and stark on both sides as Charles and his escort trekked over a low saddle, avoiding the most rugged of the mountains.

Miss MacDonald herself lay,' Kingsburgh told him, 'but where servants are laid when in my house, I never enquire anything about it. My wife is the properest person to inform you about that.'

Ferguson asked Mrs MacDonald whether she had 'laid the Young Pretender and Miss MacDonald in one bed.' 'Sir,' she answered angrily, 'whom you mean by the Young Pretender I shall not pretend to guess; but

Tarskavaig in Armadale lay within the lands of the great Skye chief Sir Alexander MacDonald.

I can assure you it is not the fashion in the Isle of Skye to lay the mistress and the maid in the same bed together.' Kingsburgh eventually admitted the involvement of Flora in the escape from Uist, and unwisely gave more information than he need have done about Charles' move to Raasay and the mainland.

On 11 July Ferguson anchored off Armadale and sent a message to Flora, asking her to come to Castleton to answer some questions a lawyer, Roderick MacDonald, wanted to put to her on behalf of MacLeod of Talisker. Donald Roy tried to warn Flora that this was a trap, but she insisted on going, and was arrested and taken aboard HMS *Furnace*.

Virtually all the participants in the escape from the Long Island were now in custody, and only the Prince remained free. When questioned Flora was so discreet she misled her inquisitors: she incriminated neither her step-father nor the MacDonalds in Uist, and gave away no information that might lead the government forces to the Prince. Campbell knew perfectly well that Clanranald and 'One-eyed' Hugh had masterminded the plot, but could prove nothing against either – which made him very angry indeed. As early as 24 July he complained about Hugh. 'This villain met me in South Uist and had the impudence to advise me against making so close a search and that if I should for some days a little desist he made no doubt of my success . . . I suspected him at the time and have given it in charge to the officers in Skye, to apprehend him.' But Hugh had already escaped into the hills. Flora was taken to London and held for a year, but she was never tried, and Kingsburgh was imprisoned in Edinburgh Castle, but not brought to trial either.

While this drama was beginning to unfold, the MacKinnons were busy at Elgol arranging for the Prince to be ferried to the mainland. He met the old chief of MacKinnon, and on the night of 4 July prepared to board a boat that had been brought to carry him to Mallaig. As he was about to step aboard he turned to Captain Malcolm suddenly and said, 'Don't you remember that I promised to meet Murdoch MacLeod at such a place?' At the byre at Scorobreck he had indeed told Raasay's son that he would rendezvous with him at Scorobreck, but had forgotten in the rush to leave Skye.

'No matter,' Malcolm assured him, 'I shall make your apology.'

'That's not enough', said the Prince. 'Have you paper, pen and ink upon you MacLeod? I'll write him a few lines. I'm obliged so to [do] in good manners.'

Writing materials were brought, and Charles sat down and wrote:

Sir, – I thank God I am in good health, and have got off as design'd. Remember me to all friends, and thank them for the trouble they have been at. – I am, Sir, your humble servant
James Thomson

Malcolm produced a pipe of tobacco and helped to light it, singeing Charles' cheek as he did so. The Prince smoked the pipe slowly, presented the Captain with a silver buckle, took him in his arms and kissed him twice and gave him 10 guineas. Then he boarded the little craft and sailed from Skye.

The letter was duly delivered to young Raasay, then passed to Donald Roy, who showed it to Kingsburgh, Lady Margaret and Flora. He then destroyed it along with the letter of safe conduct that Flora's step-father had provided for the Betty Burke journey, and one from Lady Margaret, which he had been unable to deliver to the Prince. It was as well he took these precautions, for Campbell and Ferguson arrived only a few days later and began to make their arrests. But by then the wily Donald Roy, like 'One-eyed' Hugh and the Prince, had vanished.

FROM THE ROUGH BOUNDS TO CLUNY'S CAGE

The speed with which the Hanoverian pack learned of their quarry's escape from Uist to Skye, and the deftness with which Betty was transformed back to Prince Charlie and moved to the mainland demonstrated the efficiency of intelligence gathering by both sides. Cumberland's interrogation was ruthless and effective, but suffered from always lagging at least several days and often a week or more behind the Prince's movements.

Cumberland became so angry when he learned of the escape from the Long Island that he issued a new order for the Pretender's son to be taken dead or alive. He had already stayed on in Scotland longer than intended in the hope of capturing Charles, but in July humiliation was heaped on embarrassment with intelligence that the rebel prince had escaped from Skye as well. Commodore Thomas Smith, commander of the Royal Navy in Hebridean waters, redoubled his efforts to prevent French ships from reaching Scotland, while militia and redcoats on land scoured both coast and mountains.

Charles landed at Mallaig early on the morning of 5 July, and spent three nights in the open while the MacKinnon clan chief searched for a secure hideout. On 8th John MacKinnon, the Strath laird who had escorted him from Skye, decided to move him into Loch Nevis, where he knew Clanranald was in hiding. It proved a hazardous journey: as their small boat entered the loch five men on shore 'with red crosses over their bonnets' – regular soldiers – ordered them to land. Charles was all for obeying and fighting, but MacKinnon ordered his boatmen to row like fury. He apologised later for deliberately disobeying a royal command, but Charles realised it was fortunate he had done so, for they managed to row round the point and hide the Prince on a wooded hill overlooking the loch.

On the far side of Loch Nevis, close to an island now known as the Prince's Island, Old Clanranald was in hiding. MacKinnon's meeting with the chief still rankled fifteen years later when he recounted it to Bishop Forbes from his bed in the infirmary at Edinburgh: 'When John was going to [MacDonald of] Scotus' house, he spied Clanranald . . . who, upon

The famous silver sands of Morar, to which Charles returned from Skye, were far from welcoming. After landing at Mallaig he could find nowhere to shelter so had to sleep in the open for three nights.

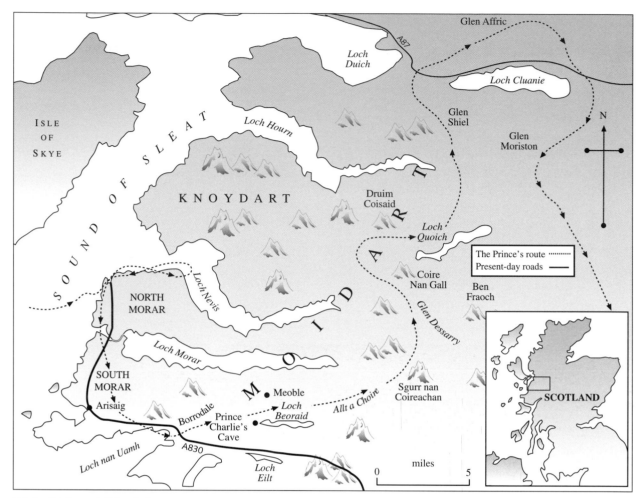

8 July–15 August. Wandering among the barren mountains and glens of the West Highlands, Charles desperately tried to make contact with a French ship but failed.

seeing John made all haste he could to get within doors,' Forbes wrote, 'but John mended his step and got hold of the tail of Clanranald's coat just as he was entering the door.'

Clanranald feigned surprise: 'O! Mr MacKinnon, is this you? I did not know you. How do you do?'

'Indeed,' John replied coldly, 'it is hard nowadays to distinguish friends from foes.'

When MacKinnon explained he had brought the Prince, the old chief's response was 'What muckle devil has brought him to this county again?' He refused to help. In retrospect this response is understandable since he and his family had been arrested and questioned on Uist and Benbecula only weeks earlier. He was free now, but had no intention of jeopardising his life or his lands again for a lost cause.

MacKinnon had witnessed the risk people like Flora MacDonald, Donald Roy and others had run without considering their own safety, and was incensed: 'If this be the best advice or opinion you have to give, Clan, you had better keep it to yourself, for the following of it would be to throw the

Prince directly into the hands of his enemies.' The Prince received the report of Clanranald's disloyalty more stoically: 'Well, Mr MacKinnon, there is no help for it. We must do the best we can for ourselves,' was his only comment.

That night the Prince walked to MacDonald of Morar's house, where he was warmly welcomed, and sent Morar in search of Young Clanranald, who was known to be in the vicinity. Morar soon returned, saying he had been unable to locate Young Clan. Morar's attitude had now changed: he had turned strangely cold, and, far from showing his earlier eagerness to help, made it clear he could do nothing. Poor Charles felt betrayed by this sudden sense of coldness that had seeped into the MacDonalds who had guarded him so loyally over the past three months.

MacKinnon refused to believe Morar's story, and spoke bitterly about the young chief. However, during succeeding weeks, when the Prince was trying to avoid capture in the mountains, Young Clanranald worked as hard as anyone to prepare a safe hiding place. At the time, however, the

Overleaf: Loch Beoraid. Hemmed in by steep hills this loch, although not far from Glenfinnan, had no road to it and was ideal country in which to hide.

The River Morar in spate.

Prince was sorely disappointed, wounded the more deeply because the Clanranald branch of Clan Donald had been so faithful in the past. 'When fortune smiled upon me and I had pay to give, I then found some people ready enough to serve me,' he told Morar bitterly, 'but now that fortune frowns on me and I have no pay to give, they forsake me in my necessity.'

Morar was persuaded at least to allow his own son to guide Charles and his friends to Borrodale beside Loch nan Uamh, and to arrange for an itinerant packman then selling his wares around the district to go to Fort Augustus to gather what intelligence he could concerning government troop movements. This gesture did not altogether soothe the Prince's ruffled feelings. He handed Morar a guinea to recompense the pedlar, and when the chief pointed out that a guinea was too much, answered tartly, 'Well then, Sir, if you think so, give him the one half and keep the other to yourself.'

Accompanied by the MacKinnon chief and John MacKinnon, and guided by Morar's son, Charles made yet another night trek across the stark hills to Loch nan Uamh, confident that his old friend Aeneas Macdonald of Borrodale would find him a refuge. It was only when he arrived there that he learned of the burning of Borrodale's house in the middle of May.

According to local tradition Prince Charlie spent two days in a cave close to the shore of the loch while Borrodale sent for his nephew Alexander MacDonald of Glenaladale to take over as guardian. Glenaladale had been wounded at Culloden. Now he came to his Prince without hesitation and became his chief support.

Leaving Charles in Borrodale's care, John MacKinnon and the MacKinnon chief set out for home, but the old man was taken that very same day, before he even left Morar, and John was arrested as soon as he set foot on Skye the following day. The arrests brought home to Prince Charlie the precariousness of his situation, and he moved at once to a more secure hide-out to await Glenaladale. This was another cave, unknown to most local people, set on a high precipice in the Borrodale woods, 4 miles to the east of the burnt-out house. And that is where Glenaladale found him.

Already there were whispers of the Prince's presence in the district, so Glenaladale immediately sent Borrodale's son out to reconnoitre for signs of the enemy. Back came word that he 'saw the whole coast surrounded by ships-of-war and tenders, as also the country by other military forces'. So that same night, 17 July, Charles fled into the mountains.

They call this area 'the Rough Bounds', and its wildness was the best ally the fugitive could have found anywhere in Scotland – its high sombre mountains divided by eerie valleys and deep, dark lochs ringed with little bays and rocky outcrops offered plenty of safe havens for a fugitive, and places where Cumberland's regular soldiers or Campbell's militiamen could be stalked and ambushed. The Rough Bounds was intimidating country for pursuer and pursued alike.

That night the Prince's party and their guides walked cautiously by the head of Loch Eilt, where they learned from one of their scouts that General Campbell was encamped not far to the north at Loch Nevis, with a combined naval and military force. The following morning, 18 July, spies brought intelligence that the General had set up an unbroken cordon from MacLeod country at the head of Loch Hourn in the north to Clan Cameron lands at the head of Loch Eil. According to Captain Alexander MacDonald's journal of the escape camps were placed 'within half a mile's distance of one another, their sentries being placed within call of one another, and patrols going about every quarter of an hour to keep their sentries alert, so that his royal highness might be surely caught should he attempt to pass through them'.

This day was significant in another way: the Duke of Cumberland handed over the taming of the Highlands to the Earl of Albemarle, who had commanded his front line at Culloden and shared his hearty dislike for all Scotsmen, loyal or disloyal. Cumberland had become increasingly frustrated by failure to capture the Stuart Prince and by a realisation that he and his troops, now committed in this godforsaken land, would be better employed fighting the French in Flanders. He could not wait to leave the Highlands, where the clansmen had been subdued but not pacified: King George's rule had been imposed all the way to the farthest islands of the west, clan lands were devastated, rebels were in flight and chiefs lay in gaol or skulked in the glens, unless they had already sailed into exile. If he had not yet taken Charles Stuart, there must be few left with any heart to fight for the cause.

And yet – and yet – reports to Cumberland's political masters in London demonstrated how far distanced he remained from final success. 'I am sorry to leave this country in the condition it is in,' he told the Duke of Newcastle, 'for all the good we have done is a little blood letting which has only weakened the madness, but not at all cured it, and I tremble for fear that this vile spot may still be the ruin of this Island and of our Family'.

'Butcher' Cumberland's last act epitomised his vindictiveness towards all clansmen, friends or enemies alike. Having made his deposition in Skye, MacDonald of Kingsburgh had been given the choice of remaining with General Campbell or being sent to Fort Augustus accompanied by his chief to plead his cause with the Duke of Cumberland. He chose the latter, which was a mistake – Cumberland was so enraged to learn that the Sleat factor had not arrived at Fort Augustus in irons that he sent a sharp reprimand to General Campbell, one of the last letters he drafted before he left Fort Augustus, and then had the poor factor manacled and carted off to Edinburgh Castle under a cavalry escort. Kingsburgh was never brought to trial, but spent a whole year in prison.

Overleaf: Loch Quoich. It was near the head of this loch that the Prince passed through the cordon of troops the Duke of Cumberland had set up from the head of Loch Hourn to the head of Loch Eil to trap him. The journey was made in darkness on 21 July, past a line of enemy soldiers so close that their conversation could be heard clearly.

Cumberland left, but the hunt in the Rough Bounds continued as government soldiers combed the hills within the cordon, and Jacobite supporters hurried from place to place carrying intelligence or letters, or simply in search of somewhere safe to hide. Both sides were playing a grim game of blind man's buff in which neither knew whom to trust: traitors, double agents and even friends were hard to identify. Coll MacDonald of Barisdale was one who bought his own freedom by turning double agent and passing information to the Hanoverians at Fort Augustus while he pretended to help the Prince.

Barely stopping for food or rest, Prince Charlie wandered among the hills for days during mid-July, often within sight of the enemy, and at times encountering friends, while Young Clanranald, on the wrong side of the cordon, tried unsuccessfully to make contact. Accompanied by Glenaladale, Glenaladale's brother and Borrodale's son the Prince struck eastwards in the hope of finding a gap in Campbell's cordon, or of turning north towards Ross-shire, from where there had come rumours of French ships.

At last the weather turned exceedingly hot, making it hard work keeping to the higher, bare slopes in order to spot enemy patrols more easily. They reached Sgurr Mhuide peak by early afternoon, and from there Glenaladale's brother was sent south to Glenfinnan in search of information. He was to rendezvous with them on the high peak of Sgurr nan Coireachan at about ten that evening, but missed them. Going warily they reached Ben Fraoch, where they were alarmed to see movement ahead a little. Carefully, Glenaladale crept forward, only to discover it was some of his own clansmen moving their animals out of reach of the militia, who were gathering at the head of Loch Arkaig. One of the clanswomen brought some milk, welcome on such a hot day, but fortunately she did not recognise the Prince, who had covered his head with a cloth and passed himself off as one of the servants.

They waited on Ben Fraoch for a while, hoping to be joined by Donald Cameron of Glen Pean who was known to be in the vicinity. However, they had to move on quickly when one of Glenaladale's men warned them that a hundred Argyllshire militiamen were at the foot of the hill on which they were hiding. Young Clanranald, who wrote an account of this part of the Prince's months among the heather, said that without their new guide they had to trust in 'the great Guide that directs all'. Certainly the 'great Guide' was on their side, for not only did they encounter Cameron of Glen Pean at Corrour by chance later the same day, but Glenaladale's brother who had missed the rendezvous at Sgurr nan Coirechan rejoined them by the following day.

This was Glen Pean's home country, so if anyone could lead the Prince through the enemy lines, he could. But it was not easy. 'They pursued their way through roads almost impassable even in daylight', he said, 'and travelling all night they came at four o'clock in the morning upon the 24th of July to a hill in the Brae of Locharkaig, called Mamnynleallum, from whence they could (without the help of a prospective glass) discern their enemy's camp, being not above a mile distant.' Glen Pean had mistaken the date: it was only the 19th, and the name Mannynleallum was a phonetic spelling of Mam (high moorland or shoulder) of Sgurr Choilean. He assured them also that this hill had been searched already so they spent the whole of the day on it. It was here that Glenaladale's brother stumbled on them.

That night Glen Pean guided them northwards until they reached Coire-nan-Gall, which lay on the borders of Glen Garry and Lochiel territory. Here they believed they might find some clansmen friends to help them, but there was no one. It was one in the morning and they were tired, so they settled down in 'a fast place' on the hill face near the head of Loch Quoich to rest. Glenaladale's brother went off in search of food, returning to warn them that enemy troops were marching up the other side of the hill. There was no escape: they had to lie low all day, and only at gloaming the next night, 20 July, did they dare to climb to the top of Druim Cosaidh to spy out the land.

Ahead they saw fires of the guard camp, but there was nothing for it but to move towards it stealthily, on hands and knees some of the time, and coming so close they could hear the voices of the soldiers quite distinctly. But they were not spotted. Glen Pean knew only one way over this mountain, and this meant scrambling over a very high rock where a spring gushed out of the cliff face and dropped more than a hundred feet into a gully. In the pitch darkness Cameron led the way and the Prince followed, with Glenaladale behind him. At the stream Charles missed his footing and would have fallen into the chasm had Cameron not caught him by the arm and grabbed the heather with his other hand to stop both of them from hurtling down the cliffside. He shouted to Glenaladale to help, and the two pulled Charles back on to the path.

They continued their climb to the summit of the next hill, where to their horror they saw another camp fire below, precisely where they intended to descend. Turning a little to the west they passed between two of the guards in the darkness; it was between one and two in the morning of 21 July, and they were through the enemy cordon. In three nights they had safely passed four enemy camps and twenty-five patrols.

A couple of miles further on they settled into a safe place near the head of Loch Hourn, where they ate what little food they had left – 'His royal highness covering a slice of cheese with oatmeal, which, though but dry fare, he ate very comfortably, and drank of the cold stream along with it,' said Alexander MacDonald. Charles was still drinking cold water straight from burns, and he had no whisky left to follow it as a chaser. All five members of the party lay there all day in a hollow in the ground,

In Glen Shiel Charles came close to the site of the battle where another Jacobite rising was defeated in 1719.

camouflaged with heather and a few birch branches, almost fainting from want of food.

They decided to head for Poolewe, from where rumours of a French ship were still reaching them. The West Highlands had been alive with reports of French attempts to make contact with the Prince for weeks, and ever since the brigantine *Bien Trouvé* made landfall at Cape Wrath, the farthest north-west point of the Scottish mainland, in mid-June these rumours intensified. Both government and fugitives spent weeks trying to make contact with it – for very different purposes! The brigantine made her base at Priest Island at the entrance to Loch Broom towards the end of June and the commander of the expedition Chevalier de Lanzière de Lancize landed with several companions to attempt to make contact with the Prince. Because the Royal Navy was so active off the Ross-shire coast the *Bien Trouvé* had to head well out into the Atlantic, where she was captured towards the end of July before she could pick up de Lancize, his men or Prince Charlie. In his book *Ships of the Forty-Five*, John S. Gibson quotes a description of the *Bien Trouvé*'s adventure, written by Chevalier de Dupont, who was on board when she was taken by the Royal Navy. The British mistook one of the young French cadets aboard for Prince Charlie, and when the lad took ill and was unable to leave his cabin, they became all the more convinced that Charles Stuart was their prisoner. When they realised their mistake they turned very bitter against the lad. 'This interlude helped amuse us for a while,' wrote Dupont, 'and, in the belief that if they thought they had the Prince they would not seek him elsewhere, we rejoiced in their mistake.'

While the *Bien Trouvé* was searched, the hunt continued on land for the men who had come ashore from the ship and most were quickly arrested, except for de Lancize himself who evaded capture and headed south towards Lochaber in a frantic search for the fugitive prince.

Unaware of what had happened to the *Bien Trouvé*, the Prince and his companions lay holed up at Glen Shiel, trying to solve their problems, not least of which was to find a guide to take them to Poolewe where they thought the Frenchmen might still be. They were short of food, so Glenaladale and John MacDonald of Borrodale went foraging and on the way fell in with a young Glen Garry lad, Donald MacDonald, whose father had been killed by government troops the previous day. Donald offered to act as guide and returned with them to the hiding place on the mountainside facing into the sun which beat down all day. They gorged their starved stomachs with butter and cheese the foragers had brought back, although it was very salty and they had nothing to wash it down or quench the thirst the salt and the hot day brought on. A stream ran only a stone's throw away, but Glen Pean would not allow anyone to risk walking to it until nightfall when they were able to drink their fill.

Loch Cluanie, lying between Glen Moriston and Glen Shiel and with high peaks to the north and south, runs for 7 miles along the road to the isles to along the road to Skye. All the time he was in this area Prince Charlie was never far from his hunters, and he had several narrow escapes.

While they were quenching their thirst the son of Gilchrist McGrath (or McKra), who had supplied the butter and cheese in the morning, appeared with a quantity of goat's milk, and gave them the news that the *Bien Trouvé* had left Poolewe. In the light of this the fugitives decided to turn east towards Glen Moriston, where their Glen Garry guide assured them he could find them shelter.

Leaving Donald Cameron behind, they set off in the clear, calm night, but had not gone far when Glenaladale realised his purse containing forty gold louis d'or belonging to Prince Charlie and five silver shillings of his own – all the money they had – was missing. He and young Borrodale walked back to where they had been camped, and found the purse, but only the five shillings remained in it. Glenaladale realised that the McGrath boy must have stolen the gold, so he walked all the way back to McGrath's house and woke him to tell him what had happened.

McGrath grabbed a piece of rope and hauled his son outside: in a great passion he brandished the rope before the boy. 'You damned scoundrel,' he shouted, 'this instant get these poor gentlemen's money . . . or by heavens I'll hing you to that very tree you see this moment.' Shivering with fear the boy retrieved the Prince's louis d'or, which he had buried close to the house. When they returned the Prince told them that he had spotted an enemy officer and three men on the opposite bank of the river Shiel, and that, but for the lost purse, they might have been captured.

Early on the morning of 23 July the Glen Garry guide led them high on to the slopes of Strathcluanie where they could feel relatively safe, although not far enough beyond the range of their enemies for peace of mind. During the afternoon they heard shooting not far off: it was probably some other poor souls being hunted down, but it could so easily have been themselves. They prudently considered that it was time to move on. There was another good reason for leaving this hillside: as the day wore on, John MacDonald of Borrodale explained, 'we greatly suffered by mitches [midges], a species of little creatures troublesome and numerous in the highlands; to preserve him [Charles] from such troublesome guests, we wrapt him head and feet in his plaid, and covered him with long heather'. Lying there Prince Charlie uttered heavy sighs and groans.

After that the trek along the high mountain ridge became almost pleasant as they followed a high hill track northwards from Glen Moriston towards Strathglass and struggled to the top of one of the peaks, probably Sgurr nan Conbhairean. But by the time they reached the summit the night had become so dark it was perilous to continue and rain had come on again, soaking the Prince to the skin, so that they were forced to stop in an uncomfortable open-fronted cave. Here they could not even make a fire, and the only comfort the Prince found was his pipe.

It was impossible to sleep, so at three in the morning Glenaladale's brother and the guide left in search of the Glen Garry lad's friends and a

Glen Moriston. Prince Charlie found refuge in the hills above this glen which now forms part of the main road from Invermoriston on Loch Ness to Kyle of Lochalsh on the west coast.

Glen Moriston hideout. Among the mountains here the Men of Glenmoriston took the Prince into their care and fed and cared for him in a cave where 'he was lulled asleep with the sweet murmurs of the finest purling stream . . . by his bedside'.

The River Cannich. Charles had to ford this fast-flowing river at Muchrachd on his return south after abandoning the plan to go to Poolewe.

The cave at Glenmoriston where the Prince was hidden by the Men of Glenmoriston, drawn by Alex Ross.

couple of hours later Charles followed to a neighbouring hill on which they had arranged to rendezvous. There the scouts returned with good news – they were to bring the fugitive and his friends to a secure place. The new guardians had no idea who was being brought to them: they suspected it might be Young Clanranald, but that did not matter to them, the man in need was a friend of the Cause and they would protect anyone from government hunters.

At Corriegoe, to the north of Loch Cluanie, the new guardians John and Alexander MacDonald and Alexander Chisholm recognised the Prince immediately because they had served in his Army. When they told their story afterwards they said that John MacDonald stopped in his tracks, 'turned as red as blood' when he saw who had been brought to them and promised to serve as loyally now as he and his friends had done in the past. The three were members of a legendary group known as the Men of Glenmoriston, who, following Cumberland's savage treatment of Glen Moriston clansmen who surrendered after Culloden, had taken a solemn oath to harry government forces wherever they found them. Along with four others – Chisholm's brothers Donald and Hugh, Patrick

Grant and Gregor MacGregor, and later a fifth, Hugh MacMillan – they spent the summer attacking and robbing redcoats. In the crudest terms they were bandits, in modern warfare terminology, guerrillas; under whatever label they operated, they were Robin Hoods who lived by their wits to help fellow Jacobites in distress and wreak the kind of vengeance that made the Highlands such a frightening place for redcoats and militia.

Grant told of rape and pillage, some of it by Skye militia, in the glen and recounted one of his group's typical ambushes. They fell on seven redcoats making their way from Fort Augustus to Glenelg one day shortly before they took the Prince into their care, shot two, and when the other five fled, they seized the bread and wine the soldiers carried. Patrick added with delight: 'O, we made a bonny bonfire of the two sogers' red coats.' His only regret was that they had finished the wine before the Prince arrived.

On the face of it, honesty may not have been their chief stock in trade, but the Men of Glenmoriston were never tempted by the £30,000 reward they could have earned so easily by betraying the Prince. The eight were men of Highland honour. They willingly took an oath of fidelity and secrecy and promised to care for the Prince, then found mutton, butter and cheese for him to eat. They had no bread, but they did have whisky, which was just as welcome. Charles suggested he should declare an oath of loyalty to them similar to theirs to him, but they refused. The Glenmoriston eight were men with minds of their own, and when he promised to look after them if ever he was restored they reminded him that Charles II had forgotten his friends when he was given back his crown.

Alexander MacDonald described the Glen Moriston cave as big enough to hold forty men, and far superior to any other in which the Prince had stayed before. In it 'he was refreshed with such chear as the exigency of the time afforded; and making a bed for him, his royal highness was lulled asleep with the sweet murmurs of the finest purling stream that could be, running by his bedside'. Here he enjoyed only three nights of peace before he had to move on yet again as intelligence told him that the Frenchman de Lancize was not far away and he decided to make for Poolewe again.

At first the Prince moved only a couple of miles or so to another cave as comfortable as the previous one, but that was too good to last. Scouts warned that the militia were only 4 miles away, so he had to push on, and by 3 August had reached Clan Chisholm country in the Strathglass valley. The following day two scouts were sent to Poolewe while the main party followed and at two in the morning on 6 August they clambered to the summit of a mountain about 40 miles short of Poolewe. Referred to by contemporaries as Peinachyrine, the mountain is usually identified today as Ben Acharain, but Sir John Ure, author of *A Bird on the Wing*, believes it

Overleaf: Glen Cannich. The most northerly point the Prince reached in his flight was near here. He had been making his way to Poolewe, where he had heard a French ship was waiting, when a message reached him to say that it had already left.

may have been Meallan Odhar, which was marked on eighteenth-century maps as Binachan. This peak was the most northerly point Prince Charlie reached in his flight.

The scouts returned with news that the only French ship that had been at Poolewe had left, but had landed two officers who were making their way to Lochiel's country in search of the Prince. This was confirmation of the *Bien Trouvé* visit and of the presence of de Lancize, who might have brought some dispatches from France for the Prince.

The next night they set out for Strathglass and crossed the Cannich water to Fasnakyle, where they hid for three days while they probed the strength of militia in the area. By 13 August the way back to Glen Moriston appeared clear, so they walked there in daylight. However, they had to take cover on learning that the enemy was searching the braes of Glen Garry. While they waited they sent a messenger to summon Cameron of Clunes.

Although the going was as hard as ever over mountain paths, through bogs and across rivers running high because of the wet summer, at least the country was now relatively clear of enemy troops. Albemarle was losing hope and Kingston's Horse had been sent south from Fort Augustus at the end of July. On 13 August, when the Prince's party was making the daytime march to Glen Moriston, Albemarle left for Edinburgh with the bulk of his forces, while many of the militia, in whom he had little faith anyway, were disbanded. Only Lord Loudoun remained with his own regiment and seventeen companies of militia. The Highlands were now much safer for Prince Charlie.

In broad daylight on 14 August the Prince, with about ten companions, trekked through Glen Moriston, Glenlyne and Glen Garry to Loch Arkaig. It was safer but no more comfortable, as they discovered when they reached the River Garry and had to wade through water that lapped their waists as they forded it. Soaking wet, cold and miserable they continued for a mile then settled down to spend the night on the open hillside. 'It rained excessively,' commented young Borrodale. In the morning, still in pouring rain, they pressed on, although by now they had no food left, so hunger compounded their misery. Fortunately, one of the Glenmoriston men shot a deer that day, which solved the problem for the time being.

That week in the vicinity of Loch Arkaig was hectic: Clunes joined them and Cameron of Lochiel's brother Dr Archie Cameron and the Reverend John Cameron, a minister; Lochiel himself, who still had not recovered fully from his Culloden wounds, remained in a hiding place on Ben Alder. It was probably here that Charles met de Lancize and a companion, a cloak and dagger encounter that came close to farce. De Lancize had found his way to Lochiel country, though heaven alone knew how since he had not a word of Gaelic. Naturally he and his attendant were suspected of being spies, and Charles was presented to them as a Captain Drummond who carried a letter from the Prince – a

Donald Cameron, 'the Gentle Lochiel', supported the Prince from the raising of the standard until the two men sailed to France together in September 1746. This portrait hangs in the Clan Cameron Museum at Achnacarry.

FRANCE AND THE '45

First port of call for the Heureux *and* Prince de Conti *when they came in search of Prince Charlie was Loch Boisdale on South Uist, among friendly MacDonald clansmen.*

Background: *Loch nan Uamh.*

Throughout the eighteenth century the French used the Jacobites as an excuse to attack Britain, or simply to tweak the lion's tail. Time after time this raised the hopes of the exiled Stuarts only to have them dashed. It was when King Louis XV abandoned an invasion plan in 1744 that Prince Charlie embarked on his 1745 rising.

Louis made much noise but provided little real support during the '45, although some ships did run the gauntlet of the British Navy and storms to carry men and arms to Scotland. Most successful was Lord John Drummond's landing with 800 men of the Royal Ecossais Regiment at Montrose on 22 November. When the campaign was going well King Louis sent the Marquis d'Eguilles to Scotland as his ambassador and signed a treaty with the Jacobites at Fontainebleau. Under this, the last military coalition to result from Scotland's Auld Alliance with France, Louis promised to help, but in return James Stuart, the Old Pretender, had to agree secretly to allow France in future to recruit his subjects to the French Army. An expedition was planned, but by the time it was ready the tide had turned and Charles had retreated from Derby partly in the belief that help was on its way from France.

King Louis XV in all his majesty – friend of the Prince's cause but slow to provide the support the '45 needed.

had no more success when she came to Loch Broom and Uist. She did not find the Prince, but picked up two of his associates, John William O'Sullivan and Felix O'Neil. The *Bien Trouvé* sailed just after the *Hardi Mendiant* and landed Chevalier de Lanzière de Lancize, who managed to contact the Prince in Lochiel's country, but the ship was captured by the Royal Navy.

At last the *Heureux* and *Prince de Conti* anchored in Loch nan Uamh on 6 September and waited there patiently while Bonnie Prince Charlie's most recent hide-out was tracked down. The Prince was brought aboard and in the early hours of 20 September the ships sailed to the Continent. France had at last been of service in Prince Charlie's attempt to win back the Stuart Crown.

The French did try again to show their support for the Jacobites by sending another well-supplied ship, the *Prince Charles*. However, at the end of March, on the eve of Culloden, it was captured with 200 men and £12,000 of much-needed money. Then through the prescience of Antione Walsh the *Mars* and *Bellone* arrived with supplies in April and fought a brief but sharp battle with three Royal Navy ships in Loch nan Uamh.

Four further rescue attempts followed. The *Levrier Volant* came to Loch Broom, but had to make a quick departure because the minister there, an ardent Hanoverian, warned Cumberland. She sailed to the Long Island, then had to flee back to France. The *Hardi Mendiant*

Still among the MacDonalds, the rescue ships made contact with the Prince at Loch nan Uamh, a loch that had played a key role in the '45.

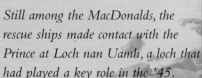

Loch Laggan. The country here was more open, but underfoot the ground was as treacherous as ever when the Prince passed by the southern end of Loch Laggan on his way to meet Cameron of Lochiel.

letter he had written himself. Exactly what role de Lancize played in the final escape is unclear, but certainly after this meeting a closer watch was kept on the west coast for French rescue ships.

In spite of all the rough living and hardship over recent weeks the Prince was in remarkably good spirits. The minister John Cameron described him as 'very cheerful and in good health, and, in my opinion, fatter than when he was at Inverness'. In appearance he looked more than ever a Highlander, still clinging to the tattered but much-loved kilt. 'He was then bare-footed, had an old black kilt coat on, a plaid, philabeg [kilt] and waistcoat, a dirty shirt and a long red beard, a gun in his hand, a pistol and durk by his side', said Cameron.

On 28 August Charles said goodbye to the Glenmoriston men, after giving them 24 guineas to share among themselves. He then set out on the 30 mile walk to Lochiel's hide-out on Ben Alder. Rather than attempt the difficult direct route, the Prince and his companions crossed the Great Glen at the southern end of Loch Lochy near Spean Bridge, then turned north almost to Fort Augustus – hazardous since there were still enemy troops there. From there they walked through the Corrieyairack Pass, where

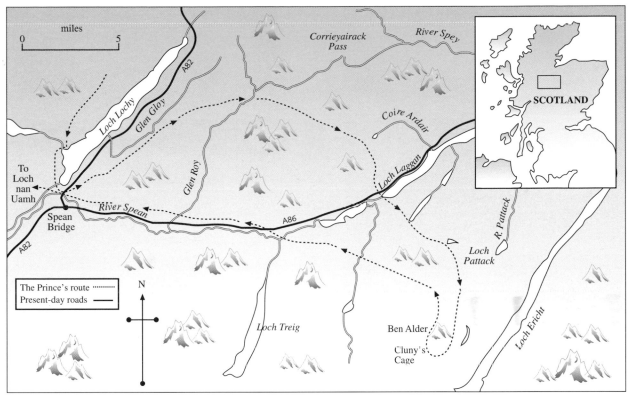

16 August–19 September. After hiding around Loch Arkaig, Prince Charlie was taken into the rugged mountains west of the Great Glen, and on to Ben Alder, where he hid in Cluny's Cage until news of rescue ships arrived. He then returned to Loch nan Uamh from where he sailed on the night of 19/20 September.

Charles' Army had scored its first success a year before, and south again by Loch Laggan to Ben Alder. It was a hard grind lasting a night and a day. On 30 August at a small sheiling on the mountain he met loyal Lochiel, whose arrival at Glenfinnan the year before had made the raising of the standard possible and who had now spent three months in hiding while his Culloden injuries healed. It was a joyful reunion with many toasts in whisky and plenty of good food, for Lochiel had been looked after well by his cousin, Cameron of Clunes, and other clan members. They spent two happy days together until Clunes decided it was time to move the Prince on.

On 5 September Macpherson of Cluny took the Prince to what was to be his last hiding place, a spacious cave at Lettermillichk set into the rocky face of Ben Alder, close to the southern end of Loch Ericht. Cluny's Cage, as it is known, was built on a steep slope and consequently was on two levels, an upper floor for living quarters and a lower one for a kitchen and store-room. Wood had been laid to make level floors, and it was thatched over with broom and furze. A large tree ran from end to end along the roof and gave it the appearance of a cage, hence its name Cluny's Cage.

The entrance to the Cage was concealed by a holly bush, and from its high position on the mountainside approaching enemy soldiers could be seen in good time. Even the hearth, which was formed from two large stones, could be used freely since the smoke from its fire was unseen against the grey rock

Loch Loyne sunset. Enemies were always close by while the Prince was in this area, but eventually they withdrew and Charles and his companions walked down the south side of the loch, and waded waist-deep across the raging River Garry.

In Glen Garry the enemy were still scouring the hillsides, although the hunt was beginning to be scaled down, and the Prince had to move with great caution.

face. Cluny's own description of the Cage was that it 'was no larger than to contain six or seven persons, four of which number were frequently employed in playing at cards, one idle looking on, one backin [baking], and another firing bread and cooking'. But there was space enough for Charles to enjoy the excellent company of Lochiel, his brother Dr Archie Cameron, Lochgarry, Cluny MacPherson and others, sharing good conversation helped along with plenty of brandy and food prepared over the fire. Lochiel was losing hope of arranging a rescue among the islands and lochs of the west coast; he proposed they should send a small party to the east to investigate the possibility of chartering a ship there to take Charles to Holland or France. At the same time as close a watch as ever was kept on the west coast.

At one o'clock on the morning of 13 September John McColvain, one of Lochiel's most trusted tenants, and Young Cameron of Clunes, guided by a Cluny clansman, Alexander McPherson, arrived at the Cage and roused the sleeping Prince. Two ships had anchored in Loch nan Uamh and were waiting to take Prince Charlie back to France.

THE LONG WALK TO FREEDOM

News that there were two large, well-armed French ships waiting in Loch nan Uamh to carry Prince Charlie back to France may appear on the surface a straightforward and logical conclusion to the '45 rising and the subsequent five-month-long flight among the heather. But the rescue of the 'rash adventurer' was far from as simple as that. This final act of the drama began months earlier, and the sequence of events leading up to it ranged as far afield as Norway and France as well as in the depths of the Scottish Highlands and the mercantile seaways beyond the north of Scotland. Its cast of characters ranged from King Louis to humble John McColvain, the man who brought the news of the arrival of the rescue ships from France to Cluny's Cage on the face of Ben Alder. Rescue lay at the end of a long and complex trail, which could easily have taken a wrong turning as had happened on previous occasions.

By July both sides faced an impasse that the most assiduous espionage and intelligence work seemed unable to overcome, a barrier apparently as impenetrable as General Campbell's ring of militia and redcoats in the mountains of Lochaber during July. Unlike the Prince's guides on that occasion, however, no one knew a way through the intelligence cordon.

The British government was still able to locate its quarry and discover the direction in which it was travelling, but always too late and never precisely enough to make a capture – just as it had been ever since the beginning of Prince Charlie's flight. Information so often reached the Hanoverian hunters too late to be of real use that one must suspect a number of men from apparently loyal clans were withholding information or passing on deliberate lies or partial truths. Cumberland left for the south, angry and frustrated. Albemarle proved no more successful, and by the end of August Lord Loudoun was left the do the best he could on land while Commodore Smith faced new problems at sea.

By this time the hunt among the isles, so intense in May and June, was scaled down, not so much due to lack of will or hope as to the fact that

The grave of Roderick MacKenzie, a young Highlander who was mistaken for Prince Charlie and murdered by Hanoverian troops, lies at the top of Glen Moriston towards Loch Cluanie.

On Ben Alder Prince Charlie's guardians found him a safe refuge on the face of 'a very rough high rocky mountain'. Here he lived in greater comfort than he had known during almost all of his five months on the wing, until word arrived that two French ships were waiting at Loch nan Uamh to take him back to France.

Commodore Smith's ships contained large numbers of prisoners who had to be taken south for trial (Flora MacDonald among them). Also, he had to divert his big ships to the far north of Scotland to protect Britain's merchant shipping, which was being devastated by French privateers. By the closing days of August this left Hebridean waters guarded only by a few sloops, and the way was clearer than it had been all summer for new rescue bids to be launched from France. John S. Gibson claims that if Commodore Smith had remained at Tobermory he would have been in a much better position to intercept any intruder arriving in search of the Prince. Removing his ships from Hebridean waters was an understandable, but vital, error of judgement on the part of a splendid naval officer.

As for the Prince's link with France, where the best hope of rescue lay, the meeting with de Lancize and the arrival and departure of the *Bien Trouvé* demonstrated how escape depended on chance rather than on any carefully laid plan. It took weeks to pass information between the Highlands and Paris. For example, the French capital did not learn of Culloden until mid-May, and communication became worse during Prince Charlie's months on the wing. O'Sullivan, who was picked up by the French ship *Le Hardi Mendiant* on 5 July, did not arrive in Paris until 15 September after an adventurous journey via Norway and Holland.

By July loyal clan chiefs were beginning to think about searching for a secure place in Scotland where the Prince might spend the winter, and at the same time alarm was growing in Paris because summer was passing and it would be dangerous to send ships into stormy Scottish waters during autumn or winter. King Louis had provided precious little help during the campaign, not so much due to lack of enthusiasm for the rising but more because of political infighting in Paris and inefficiency in organising an expedition. Individual ships trying to carry men, money or arms seldom arrived because they were intercepted by the ever vigilant Royal Navy.

After Culloden the will to rescue the Prince remained strong, but France was handicapped by lack of information about how or where to locate him. Those who returned aboard the *Mars* and *Bellone* were of little help, and a coyly coded letter sent by O'Sullivan from Bergen to the Pretender's agent in Paris on 15 July took the best part of two months to reach its destination. In this thinly disguised message, O'Sullivan described the events following Culloden. Pretending that

Flora's grave at Kilmuir, Skye, serves as a reminder of the loyalty of the clans during Prince Charlie's flight.

From Ardnamurchan Point French ships sailed into Loch nan Uamh.

Charles was a shipwrecked merchant he wrote: 'My associate [Charles] and I after our unlucky shipwreck of the 15th of April last [he meant Culloden on the 16th], retreated into a spot where we hoped to be able to collect a little of the remains of our property and to try and reestablish our business as far as was possible and thus to give time to our correspondent in France to arrange our affairs with our creditors and to extricate us from the awkward situation in which we were.' He described the wanderings in the Outer Isles and how his 'associate' would have fallen into creditors' (Hanoverian) hands but for 'the help of a lady who transformed my associate and conveyed him to Heaven [Skye]'. He then put forward a plan to rescue the fugitive with the help of Mr Adam (King Louis).

But by the time this letter and O'Sullivan himself reached Paris 'Mr Adam' had set his own plan in motion: in utmost secrecy two privateers, the *Heureux*, which carried 36 guns and 275 men, and her slightly smaller companion the *Prince de Conti*, with 30 guns and 225 men, were fitted out to sail to Scotland to seek Prince Charlie and bring him back to France. The expedition was under the command of Colonel Richard Warren with Old Tom Sheridan's nephew Michael, who had returned with the *Mars/Bellone* expedition, among those who accompanied him.

The Frenchmen made landfall at Barra Head on 4 September and moved straight to Loch Boisdale, intent on finding MacDonald of Boisdale, who was well known in France to be a sympathiser and as likely as anyone to hold the key to finding the Prince. A large force from the two ships landed on South Uist, and marched on Boisdale's home at Kilbride only to find the chief was still in gaol and unable to help. However, there was someone else who could – unnamed, but probably Rory MacDonald who had rowed the Prince from the mainland to Benbecula and back to Skye, and who knew these waters well enough to pilot the French ships to Clanranald's mainland country of Moidart and Arisaig. In a storm that was driving smaller vessels to seek shelter the *Heureux* and *Prince de Conti* were piloted across the Minch into Loch nan Uamh, where they dropped anchor on Friday 6 September. The only other vessel in the loch was a little cargo ship called the *May*, but the Frenchmen flew British colours at their mast just in case the Royal Navy spotted them.

Carrying a much needed shipment of oatmeal from Glasgow to the West Highlands, the *May* had been caught in a fierce storm off Ardnamurchan Point and forced to run for shelter in Loch nan Uamh. Her captain, Lachlan MacLean, watched the newcomers warily because Royal Navy patrols were not to be trusted and could treat British merchant ships' masters on the Scottish west coast as roughly as enemy captains. To MacLean's great alarm, one of the big ships sent a small boat over and boarded him. He told the British authorities when questioned later: 'After they came to anchor they sent their boat with 16 men, boarded our vessell, told us we were prisoners of war in the French King's name, carried us all on board their largest ship, called the *Happy* frigate, commanded by Captain Boullue.'

The unlucky Captain was taken before Warren, who acted and talked extravagantly about his mission. 'He took an inventory of our ship and cargo and money, put six of their men on board our vessel and one officer,' MacLean said. And for the next fortnight every man aboard the *May* remained a prisoner.

Unknown to Warren the boarding and arrest of the Scottish captain was being watched by Aeneas MacDonald of Borrodale and his sons Ranald and John, who had taken to the moors above Borrodale when they saw the 'British' ships anchor. From their hiding place they watched the arrest of the *May*, but summoned up courage to send someone aboard to find out what these ships were doing in the loch. Donald MacDonald, an Edinburgh tailor who was travelling in this part of the country to collect money owed by local lairds, was at Borrodale at this time – a man in whom John MacDonald said 'we hade great confidence'. MacDonald was sent out to the *Heureux* under the pretext of offering his tailoring services to the ships' officers, and on the ship he and Young Clanranald, who accompanied him, met Michael Sheridan, whom Clanranald knew well.

Clanranald and the tailor returned with the joyous news that the ships were French and had come in search of the Prince. The next day French officers came ashore and paid a visit to Borrodale at the hut in which the chief and his family had been living since their home had been burned down. Young Borrodale described their arrival at the hut:

After nightfall twelve french, with two officers at their hade [head] came to a smal hut we repaired sometime before that for our own reception, as all our houses before that were all burned; the names of the officers were jung Sheridan and Capn O'Neil, who at their arrival, enquired for us all, as they knew us weel formerly, and wished much to have some discourse of consequence with us. Upon our being informed of this, we appeared, and after a long conversation were convinced of their sincerity, and oblidged them to produce their credentials from France, before we revealed any parte of our secrets to them.

In the environment of duplicity and double dealing in the Highlands at this time one could never be too careful.

It was inevitable that news of the *Heureux* and *Prince de Conti* and their mission should soon spread: in fact, no sooner had the ships touched land in the Hebrides than word was on its way to Lord Loudoun at Fort Augustus, but for some strange reason it did not reach the Hanoverian

Overleaf: Here at Loch nan Uamh the Prince first landed on the Scottish mainland, from here he sailed to the Outer Hebrides to take refuge after Culloden, and this was the place from which he sailed to safety in September 1746.

leader until Thursday 18 September. Why so long? News from the islands would normally pass to Fort Augustus within a few days, so one can only guess that the delay on this occasion was due either to lack of co-ordination between the Navy and the Army, or that it had been deliberately held back. If the latter, then the obvious suspects are those friends of the Cause who served in the militia.

Another spy was soon at large, however: the tailor in whom John MacDonald of Borrodale had such confidence went straight to Edinburgh and gave a full account of his activities to Lord Albemarle. He told the Commander-in-Chief that discussion of the rescue plan on board ship had been open and frank when he and Young Clanranald visited the *Heureux*. The French had been in great fear up to that moment, he said, lest they might fail to make contact with the Prince, and were actually contemplating leaving the west coast to sail through the Pentland Firth to ask about him at a friendly house near Stonehaven, which of course was good Jacobite territory. The tailor was prepared to name names, and added that the French were contemplating sailing as far south as Edinburgh in order to enquire about Prince Charlie at the houses of Norwell Hume near Bathgate, Lady Bruce in Leith and Lady Cunningham at Priestfield. Fortunately, all these useful titbits of information came too late.

Due to bungling or deliberate delays, the *Heureux* and *Prince de Conti* were able to lie in Loch nan Uamh unmolested from 6 to 19 September with the foul weather their best ally. Day after day, according to the logs of the *Heureux* and *Conti*, friendly winds carrying squally showers kept other ships away, but when these storms died back briefly one day, the Frenchmen were able to make a quick foray into the open sea to spy out for other shipping. They saw none, so returned to the calmer waters of the loch where the master of the *May* sat miserably idle. 'We hourly looked in vain for deliverance from our ships of war,' he wailed, 'but to our grief none appeared.'

While Highland leaders visited the ships, many trying to arrange passages to safety for themselves, the hunt began to locate the Prince. That summer the Highlands had been a place of no secrets and of many secrets: Prince Charlie's safety had depended upon a 'need to know' policy among the clans, which ensured that as soon as one guardian handed him on to another, he had no idea where Charles had gone or into whose care he was eventually passed. As a result people like John MacDonald of Glenaladale, who had been so involved in the chase during July and August, had little knowledge of where to search in September. He guessed the Prince would be in Cameron's care, so he set out for Glenfinnan and Lochiel's country around Achnacarry, where he had handed the Prince over to Cameron of Clunes only a month earlier.

Luck still played its part: Glenaladale was fortunate enough to meet an old clanswoman who was able to confirm that the fugitive was with

Lochiel in Badenoch. So, while Clunes' son was sent to Badenoch, Glenaladale returned to Loch nan Uamh to make sure the French ships did not leave without the Prince. Chance continued to play its part: as young Clunes walked towards Badenoch, accompanied by John McColvain, he encountered Lochiel's brother Dr Archie Cameron and MacPherson of Cluny on their way back from Ben Alder, and they were able to direct the searchers to Cluny's Cage. Guided by Alexander McPherson, Clunes and McColvain reached the hide-out in the middle of the night of Friday 13 September.

Within an hour Charles was on the march, accompanied by Lochgarry and Lochiel, who was now well enough to travel. They walked until daybreak when they rested and lay low all day in the 'superlatively bad and smockie' hut at Uiskchiltra in which the Prince had stayed less than a fortnight before. Here MacPherson of Breakachie and John Roy Stewart (always nicknamed 'The Body' for some unexplained reason) joined him. The two had abandoned their mission to charter a boat on the east coast.

Charles was in such high spirits at the prospect of escape that he played a trick on Stewart, whom he knew well. An onlooker at the reunion said that as John Roy approached he hid under a plaid and waited: 'In the door of the hut there was a pool or puddle, and when John Roy Stewart just was entering, the Prince peeped out of the plaid, which so surprised John Roy that he cried out, "O Lord! My master!" and fell down in the puddle in a faint.' From then on spirits rose, and after another night march they spent part of the day holding a shooting competition with bonnets thrown into the air as targets. Needless to say, all the participants agreed that Charlie was the best shot among them.

Because of danger of redcoat patrols still operating among the mountains and the fact that the journey took them close to Fort Augustus they could not take a direct route to Loch nan Uamh, but had to cover well over 60 miles – and move at a fast pace in case the French ships left without the Prince. They continued to travel under cover of darkness, or as much darkness as there was under the clear skies and almost full moon of that week in September. Rivers and burns were still in spate because of the heavy rain that had been falling all summer, so the prospect of crossing the River Lochy was a daunting one. They could only find a very leaky boat (the sole vessel the redcoats had not destroyed), but, fortified with three bottles of brandy spirited out of Loudoun's stores in Fort Augustus by an anonymous Jacobite sympathiser, the crossing was made without difficulty.

Arrival at Lochiel's burnt-out house at Achnacarry on 16 September must have brought home to Prince Charlie again the devastation his 'rash adventure' had heaped upon the Highlands, but his hosts made him as comfortable as they could. The following day he moved on to the head of Loch Arkaig, where Cluny and Dr Cameron met him with provisions

THE LUCKLESS HOUSE OF STEWART

The Stewart dynasty's origins lay among heroes: their end was mired in the lonely exile of Bonnie Prince Charlie and his brother Cardinal Henry of York. In between lay four centuries of unbroken tragedy. First Stewart King of Scots, Robert II, was the son of Marjorie, daughter of the hero-king Robert the Bruce and her husband Walter, High Steward of Scotland. For three-and-a-half centuries from Robert II's accession in 1371 the Stewarts ruled Scotland, and for more than a century

The plaque marking the site of Fotheringhay.

England as well. When James VII and II fled to France after the Glorious Revolution in 1688 the Stewarts 'reigned' for another hundred years in exile, and those who remained faithful to them became known as Jacobites. Because the French language does not recognise the letter 'w' the name of the royal family was changed from Stewart to Stuart when Mary Queen of Scots grew up in France and married the Dauphin. Throughout the dynasty's 450 years it was plagued by struggles against rebellious nobles, religious and social upheaval at home and war with the 'auld enemy' England, or sometimes all of these at the

The site of Fotheringhay Castle, Northamptonshire, where Mary Queen of Scots was executed in 1587.

same time. Seven monarchs in succession, from James I to James VI, succeeded as minors, half a dozen met violent deaths, including Mary Queen of Scots and Charles I, who were beheaded. Hardly surprisingly, another, King James V, died of a broken heart.

However, James VII and II never gave up hope of being restored to his throne, but every attempt failed. In 1714 the dynasty was supplanted by the Elector of Hanover, a descendant of James VI's daughter, and he became George I. In exile, however, the

The Palace of Holyroodhouse.

Stuarts continued to fight for the crown they believed to be theirs by Divine Right: the 'succession' passed from James VII and II to his son James, the Old Pretender, and in time to his grandson Charles Edward, the Young Pretender. Both led unsuccessful risings, the last and best remembered being that of 1745, when the Jacobite movement was crushed for ever at Culloden. Charles succeeded as King Charles III in 1766, and at his death in 1788 his brother Henry styled himself King Henry IX. But Henry never even tried to win back his throne, so the claim died with him in 1807.

Background: *Linlithgow Palace, birthplace of Mary Queen of Scots.*

A cairn marks the place on the shore of Loch nan Uamh where Prince Charlie went aboard the French ships that were to take him to safety at the end of his five-month-long flight.

they had laid in, and two days later Charles stood on the shore of Loch nan Uamh and gazed with joy on the ships that were waiting to take him to safety. For Colonel Warren the Prince's arrival brought a huge sense of relief that two anxious weeks of waiting, always in fear of an attack by the Navy as had befallen the *Mars* and *Bellone*, were over.

Although the master of the *May* did not actually witness the Prince's arrival, he realised something important was afoot. 'About six in the evening, after sitting to supper, a message came from the *Prince de Conti*,' he said, 'upon which Colonel Warren and the captain of the frigate got up in a great hurry, got on their best clothes, ordered us on board our vessell with our chests, where we remained guarded by their men and an officer until two next morning, the 20th, when Colonel Warren and one of his officers came on board of us ... he was in top spirits, telling us plainly that he had now got the Prince on board with Lochiel.'

Prince Charlie was taken on board the *Prince de Conti* first, then transferred to the larger *Heureux*, and within hours Warren was ready to sail. In addition to Lochiel, the Frenchmen took close on a couple of dozen Highland chiefs or gentleman – among them Lochiel's brother Dr Archie, Lochgarry and John Roy Stewart – and more than a hundred men 'of common rank'. Cluny MacPherson, MacPherson of Breakachie and 'Spanish John' MacDonald of Scotus, one of the Glen Garry family, could all have gone too, but decided to return to their clansmen although they had served the Cause well and deserved to escape. They hoped one day to prepare the clans for Charles' return.

Less deserving, but more anxious than anyone to seize this chance of freedom, was another Glen Garry chief, Coll MacDonnell of Barisdale, who had acted as a double agent during Prince Charlie's campaign and time in hiding. The moment he heard of the arrival of the *Heureux* and *Prince de Conti* Barisdale rushed to Moidart to secure a passage and succeeded, but not as he planned: Warren put him aboard the *Prince de Conti* in manacles and took him to France, where he lay in jail until 1749. Barisdale returned to Scotland only to be thrown into the dungeons of Edinburgh Castle, where he died ungrieved for the following year. 'Six soldiers, with no mourners, carried his bulky and corpulent carcase to a grave at the foot of the talus of the Castle,' wrote Bishop Forbes of his end.

On the loch shore the Prince made a little speech to those who were remaining behind, urging them to live in good hopes and assuring them that he expected to return soon 'with such a force as would enable him to reimburse us for our losses and trouble'. With that he went on board and wrote a last letter to Cluny, who was staying behind. 'Thanks to God I am arrived safe aboard the vessell, which is a very clever one, and has another alonst with her as good, the first is of 36 guns and the second 32.' He ordered payments to be made to a number of the faithful: £150 to Glen Garry's clansmen, £300 to Lochiel's and £100 each to the MacGregors

Wind ruffles the waters of Loch Arkaig just beyond the Dark Mile where the Prince found several hiding places in Clan Cameron country during his flight.

and Stewarts. Cluny himself was awarded £100 and another £100 was to be given to the widow of MacDonald of Keppoch, who had fought and died bravely at Culloden.

At two o'clock on the morning of 20 September, under the light of a full moon that hung high in a clear sky, sails were unfurled and anchors raised and the *Heureux* and *Prince de Conti* edged down the loch like ghosts into the Sound of Arisaig and disappeared from sight. As the sun rose astern next morning the *Heureux* and *Prince de Conti* passed Eigg and Muck on the starboard beam and Coll to port. The captains set their course westward, far out into the Atlantic where they could feel as safe from British men-of-war as possible.

The storms of the past months had abated at last to make a peaceful end to Prince Charlie's bloody adventure, but for the clanspeople he left behind the suffering was not over. The way of life they had known for centuries was to continue to change, and as time passed Prince Charlie and the Jacobites became little more than a memory of the dynasty that had been Scotland's for 400 years.

EPILOGUE

John MacDonald of Borrodale listened to Prince Charlie's little speech on the shore of Loch nan Uamh, urging the clans to live 'in good hopes' and promising to return, then, as he watched the French ships sail, added his own bleak thought, 'And [he] left us all in a worse state than he found us.'

That is undeniable. By the time Charles left Scotland the first of his soldiers had already been brought to trial and many were executed or banished to the colonies beyond the Atlantic. Hundreds more lay in the filthy holds of ships awaiting King George's justice, while disease speeded up the process of the law – 700 disappeared from official records, 'fate unrecorded'. In the Highlands the guilty and innocent were hunted down and many were murdered by Cumberland's troops. Those whose lives were spared had their homes burned, cattle stolen and ploughs needed to till their soil for the next year's crop wrecked. In the longer term the clan way of life was destroyed, with chiefs no longer behaving like paternal leaders but as landlords, often motivated by greed and expediency.

The London government had dealt brutally with Jacobite supporters after earlier risings, so this was a new order that Charles Stuart should have foreseen. But Charles believed he was pursuing a legitimate claim to the Crown that had belonged to his family by divine right for four-and-a-half centuries, and the possibility of defeat had never entered his head.

Charles has been accused of neither offering an apology nor showing remorse for the distress the '45 caused, yet such gestures as the payment of £100 to Keppoch's widow and that brief note sent to Donald Roy MacDonald after Flora escorted him over the sea to Skye speak volumes. It would have been too dangerous for the Prince to cite names or places, so all he was able to say in this letter was, 'Make my compliments to all those to whom I have given trouble.' That surely is acknowledgement of what they had done for him.

The Prince must have heard stories of Cumberland's depredations during the course of his flight, and certainly Captain Malcolm MacLeod spelled out the atrocities after Culloden to him while they walked from Portree to Elgol, but without seeing the actual destruction with his own eyes it would have been hard to comprehend its scale. Uist, Skye and the remoter parts of the west where he hid remained virtually unscathed, and he stayed only one night on Raasay, so would have seen little of the devastation there. On the mainland he saw the burned-out ruins of Borrodale House and Lochiel's home at Achnacarry, but little else. Nonetheless, he was troubled enough in his mind to sit wrapped up in his own thoughts for long periods at Corodale, and to start up in his sleep after his return from Raasay, crying out, 'O poor England! O poor England!' It would have been difficult though for Charles Stuart to place all the events of the previous year into any reasonable perspective during his months 'on the wing': with redcoats and militia at his heels there was time to think of little apart from where the next safe hiding place might be found.

Charles displayed astonishing stamina and courage to make long marches, usually in darkness, across bare hillfaces strewn with boulders and across bracken-covered glens and through treacherous bogs. Rivers and burns presented no obstacle, even without the comfort of Lord Loudoun's stolen brandy which fortified him for crossing the River Lochy on his way to join the *Heureux* and *Prince de Conti*. At sea he faced dangerous night voyages in fierce storms with equanimity too – apart from that first wild voyage to Benbecula soon after Culloden when he begged to be put ashore. He accepted the cold, the wetness, and the dangers of rocky Hebridean coasts stoically.

Days on end were spent in smoke-filled huts or makeshift shelters without even the comfort of a fire to dry rain-soaked clothes, and he slept in the open air among the heather when he had to. Yet he was always able to lie down and catnap for a few hours, as he had been used to doing in Rome, before moving on. The summer of 1746 was atrocious – almost constant wind and rain and none of the mellow Italian warmth to which he had been accustomed all his life – yet he never complained.

Prince Charlie relished dressing and living as a clansman, and when given a new kilt boasted that all he needed now was the 'itch' to become a true Highlander. Soon he had that, too, but made no complaint while Captain MacLeod picked four score of lice off his body during their walk through the Cuillins of Skye. To survive all that with no physical ailment other than 'a bloody flux' (diarrhoea) and no mental affliction other than occasional mood swings was an achievement in itself. To retain a sense of camaraderie and humour such as no Stuart ever displayed before was little short of miraculous. Captain Alexander MacDonald summed up all these qualities which created the legendary Prince Charlie in flight: 'His magnanimous spirit bore all crosses and adversities with the greatest Christian resignation and manly courage.'

Why then was the remainder of Prince Charlie's life such a tragedy for the Jacobites, for Scotland and for the man himself? In a word – *disappointment*. Charles intended to return, but was let down by France, Spain, followers of the Cause in England and many in Scotland as well.

Overleaf: Under a harvest moon on the night of 19–20 September 1746 Prince Charlie sailed out of a calm Loch nan Uamh, leaving behind a legend.

Nobody would help, and he simply could not cope with failure. From being Europe's hero, adulated to a degree difficult for us to comprehend today, he deteriorated into its 'Wild Man' – a ghost figure rushing from country to country, from hope to hopelessness. Charles felt betrayed by his father and his brother, who put an end to Stuart claims by becoming a cardinal of the Roman Catholic Church, and thereafter he sank into a state of brutal cantankerous alcoholism. Yet he continued to pursue schemes to recapture his throne, none of which came to anything.

The Prince's personal life turned into a succession of unsatisfactory love affairs every one of which ended disastrously, even that with Clementine Walkinshaw, who gave him a daughter whom he loved dearly. Following ceaseless quarrels, Clementine fled with their child, leaving Charles lonely and bitter. On his father's death he returned to Rome and proclaimed himself King Charles III, but in spite of a dynastic marriage, which also failed, he left no heir other than Clementine's daughter.

Charles Stuart died on the last day of January 1788. His life had progressed from being the spoilt child of his parents' unhappy marriage to tragic, drunken old man who reigned in Rome as king of nowhere. But in between there had been that gloriously rash but brave adventure to recapture his inheritance in 1745. And those five months as a fugitive among the mountains and islands of Scotland, out of which emerged the legend of Bonnie Prince Charlie.

IN PRINCE CHARLIE'S FOOTSTEPS – PLACES TO VISIT

Much of Prince Charlie's route may be traced relatively easily by car or on foot, although the wild mountainous core of the West Highlands remains as remote as it was in 1746. Because of ferry routes to the Hebrides and the ease of travelling by the road bridge linking Skye to the mainland, it is more practical not to attempt to follow the route exactly as the Prince travelled it, especially if time is limited. This itinerary takes in many of the places he saw and crosses the kind of terrain over which he travelled and where he hid during his five months in flight.

From Culloden battlefield the B851 and B862 roads pass south along Strathnairn and Stratherrick, by Gorthlick, to Fort Augustus. The A82 then leads to Invergarry, following the opposite shore of Loch Lochy to the one along which Charles rode. Just before Spean Bridge the B8004 and B8005 branch off to Achnacarry, from where it is possible to drive along the north side of Loch Arkaig. Near the end of the loch where the Prince abandoned his horse because the going became too difficult the motorist must turn back and follow the B8004 south to Fort William, which Prince Charlie had to avoid because it was garrisoned by enemy troops. The town is not to be missed by today's traveller. From Fort William the A830 leads westward by Glenfinnan and Loch nan Uamh to Mallaig.

The once-weekly Caledonian MacBrayne ferry from Mallaig to Lochboisdale on South Uist follows the Prince's route to the Outer Hebrides most closely, although it arrives at the southern end of South Uist, much further south than Rossinish, where Charles landed. A more interesting and practical route from Mallaig to the islands would be to take the regular short car ferry from Mallaig to Armadale on south Skye, then drive northward through the Sleat peninsula by way of the Museum of the Isles and with a possible detour to Elgol. The road from Elgol to Uig follows the Prince's route roughly, but in the reverse direction. It does, however, allow one to savour the glory of the peaks of the Cuillins, to see Portree and pass Kingsburgh, where the fugitive prince spent his first night on the island. From Uig a good ferry service operates to Lochmaddy on North Uist.

Whether the voyage to the Long Island is made by Lochboisdale in South Uist or Lochmaddy in North Uist, the A865 road runs all the way from the one port to the other – the length of the two Uists and Benbecula. It passes Flora MacDonald's birthplace, the Clanranald chiefs' ancient home at Ormiclett on South Uist and their more recent seat at Nunton on Benbecula. Although the islands are now linked by road rather then the tidal fords of Prince Charlie's time, this route gives a good impression of the bare, loch-pitted landscape through which the fugitive travelled and where he hid in the remote uplands between the peaks of Hecla and Ben More. At the southern end of South Uist a short detour by the B888 is well worthwhile to savour the magnificent vistas across the Sound of Barra to the islands of Barra and Eriskay, on which the Prince first landed in 1745. Ferries link North Uist with Harris, where the A859 runs through the moorland and loch-strewn landscape of Harris and Lewis all the way to Stornoway.

It is possible to return from Stornoway to Ullapool on the mainland or from Tarbert to Uig on Skye, but to experience the voyage Flora MacDonald made over the sea to Skye with the Prince disguised as her maid, Betty Burke, take the return Caledonian MacBrayne ferry from Lochmaddy back to Uig.

On Skye the drive by the A855 north from Uig gives a glimpse of Prince's Point, on the shore of Loch Snizort, where he landed. Only a few miles further north the ruin of Monkstadt House can be seen, lying a little way off the road. This was the home of the chief of Sleat, and it was here that Flora brought the news of his arrival. A few miles further on is Kilmuir, where Flora MacDonald is buried, with the Skye Museum of Island Life close by. It is possible to continue round the Trotternish peninsula to Portree, after which, instead of continuing all the way south to the Sleat peninsula, one can return to the mainland by way of the Skye road bridge at Kyleakin.

Back on the mainland the A87 passes Loch Duich and through Glen Shiel to Loch Cluanie, between mountains, whose starkness shows all too clearly the harshness of the terrain across which the Prince trekked and at times had to sleep in the open air in rain or sun. To the south lies Loch Quoich, where he escaped from Cumberland's net. Beyond Loch Cluanie the A887 branches off to the left into Glen Moriston, where Roderick MacKenzie was murdered, and it is worth pausing at his memorial cairn and grave. This was the area where the Men of Glenmoriston took the Prince into their care and concealed him. At Invermoriston the road reaches Loch Ness and branches northwards along the loch shore as the A82 to Inverness.

Off the beaten track all along the route, and in the mountain mass to the west of Ben Nevis, hill walkers with Prince Charlie's stamina can follow the route in more detail. Be warned, however, land in any particular area may be privately owned and permission may be needed; check with the local tourist centre before setting out.

PLACES TO VISIT

Along the way there are a number of museums, visitor centres and places of interest of direct relevance to the Prince's flight. And of course there are others of more general interest, which, for example, provide glimpses of the way of life following Culloden and the clearances of crofters from their clanlands. Local tourist offices will have information about how to reach these and the opening times where appropriate.

On the Mainland
Clan Cameron Museum, Achnacarry, Spean Bridge, Inverness-shire. This small museum is situated close to the home of Lochiel, the Chief of Clan Cameron, in the heart of an area where Prince Charlie had several hiding places. It contains artefacts relating to the Prince and the Jacobites, as well as 'the Gentle Lochiel', the chief who played a major part in the uprising and accompanied the Prince when he finally left Scotland for France. The museum also has exhibits about the clan regiment, the Queen's Own Cameron Highlanders, and the commandos who trained at Achnacarry during the Second World War.

Clan Macpherson Museum, Main Street, Newtonmore, Inverness-shire. History and records of Clan Macpherson and Badenoch. Cluny

MacPherson played an important part in Prince Charlie's escape, and his last hiding place was Cluny's Cage on Ben Alder.

Culloden Battlefield, near Inverness. Much has been restored to its appearance on 16 April 1746, when Cumberland defeated Prince Charlie's Army. Old Leanach Cottage, clan graves, the Well of the Dead, the Cumberland Stone and memorial cairn bring the battle to life and the National Trust for Scotland's visitor centre has a permanent exhibition of weapons and artefacts associated with the rising.

Glenfinnan Monument and Visitor Centre, Glenfinnan. The monument to mark the raising of the Stuart standard at the start of the '45 on 19 August 1745 stands on the Fort William–Mallaig road at the head of Loch Shiel. The monument, in the care of the National Trust for Scotland, affords magnificent views of Loch Shiel, and the visitor centre includes exhibitions on Glenfinnan and the '45 and the Jacobite campaign, with commentary in six languages.

Inverness Castle. Inverness, capital of the Highlands, was Prince Charlie's headquarters immediately before the Battle of Culloden. The original ancient fortress was destroyed by Prince Charlie's Army in 1746, and the present building dates from the first half of the nineteenth century. On the castle esplanade stands a statue to Flora MacDonald.

Loch nan Uamh. Every person who wants to feel a sense of the history of the '45 must spend time at this sea loch on the A830 between Glenfinnan and Mallaig. Prince Charlie first landed on the mainland of Scotland here, and at nearby Borrodale House he persuaded clan chiefs to support him, and the last battle of the rising was fought on the loch. And it was here that the Prince embarked on the night of 19/20 September 1746 and sailed back to France. A cairn marks this historic spot.

Roderick MacKenzie's memorial cairn and grave. A mile or so along the A887 on the way from Skye, as it enters Glen Moriston, a cairn on the right side of the road marks the spot where the young clansman Roderick MacKenzie was mistaken for Prince Charlie and murdered by Hanoverian soldiers. MacKenzie's grave is on the left side of the road, out of sight, down by the river.

West Highland Museum, Cameron Square, Fort William. One of the most important museums in the West Highlands, and – appropriately – it reflects all aspects of life in the region, including its Jacobite connections. The museum contains a unique collection of Jacobite artefacts, papers and portraits. These range from a secret mirror-portrait of the Prince to Jacobite drinking glasses.

On Skye

Armadale Castle Gardens and Museum of the Isles, Armadale, Sleat, Isle of Skye. Flora MacDonald's step-father, 'One-eyed' Hugh MacDonald, was tenant at Armadale in 1746, and it was here after her return to Armadale having escorted the Prince to Skye that Flora was arrested. Although Charles never visited Armadale, the area has close Jacobite connections. The museum tells the story of Clan Donald, and displays portraits and artefacts relating to the Jacobite Cause. It also contains an excellent Jacobite library, beautiful gardens and holiday cottages to rent.

Aros-Skye Heritage Centre, near Portree, Isle of Skye. This exhibition comprises a series of rooms tracing life on Skye from Culloden onwards. It includes the battle, Prince Charlie's landing on Skye, his visit to MacNab's inn at Portree and the disastrous effects of the repression and social change on the island that resulted from the '45.

Dunvegan Castle, Dunvegan, Skye. Dunvegan has been the home of the Clan MacLeod chiefs for 800 years, and claims to be the oldest inhabited castle in northern Scotland. It houses many items of interest including the clan's greatest treasures – the Fairy Flag with miraculous powers, the unique 400-year-old

Dunvegan Cup, a lock of Prince Charlie's hair cut by Flora MacDonald, the heroine's pin-cushion and a pair of spectacles that belonged to Prince Charlie's boatman, Donald MacLeod of Gualtergill.

Skye Museum of Island Life, Kilmuir, North Skye. This group of seven thatched cottages situated close to Flora MacDonald's grave illustrates island life in the past, with croft house, weaving shed, ceilidh house, smithy and barn. The museum is packed with interesting documents and artefacts. Among the most fascinating are newspapers relating to the clearances of the century following the Prince's rising, when thousands – including Flora MacDonald – were driven out of Scotland to find new lives on the other side of the Atlantic.

On the Outer Hebrides

Taigh-tasgaidh Chill Donnain, South Uist. This is also known as the museum at Kildonan (its English name) and is situated less than a mile from Flora MacDonald's birthplace at Milton on South Uist. It is an attractive small museum incorporating videos and interpretation of island life, with emphasis on the heroine's story. Behind it lie the hills with the shieling at which Flora and Prince Charlie met. It also includes a craft centre, café and performance space.

Library and Resource Centre, Liniclate School, Liniclate, Benbecula. Public library and resource centre offering tourist information and census material relating to Benbecula and the Uists. No specific Jacobite material, but of interest to anyone with Hebridean blood in search of their ancestors.

Museum nan Eilean, Stornoway, Isle of Lewis. This museum runs major thematic exhibitions of Hebridean life, and while their content is not specifically Jacobite, they give a good background to the islands among which the Prince hid. A cairn close to the harbour at Stornoway marks Prince Charlie's visit to Lewis.

Nunton Steadings, Nunton, Benbecula. This centre, opened in 2000 by the Nunton Steadings Trust, includes an exhibition of the history of the MacDonalds of Clanranald in Uist, with references to Prince Charles Edward's time spent on the islands. It also contains wildlife and natural history displays. Nunton Steadings are situated close to the former home of the Clanranald chiefs and just a few miles from Rossinish, where the Prince Charlie landed on the Long Island. At Nunton Clanranald and his wife helped to arrange the Prince's escape over the sea to Skye dressed as Betty Burke, and it was there that 'Lady Clan' and Flora sewed his maid's disguise.

Taigh Chearsabhagh, Lochmaddy, North Uist. To discover the historic and artistic life of the Outer Hebrides today a visit to this growing museum and arts centre close to the harbour at Lochmaddy is well worthwhile. Situated in a restored and extended old building, Taigh Chearsabhagh is a centre for exhibitions and working artists.

FURTHER READING

On board the *Heureux* bound for France, Prince Charlie recounted his own story of his flight to Dr Archibald Cameron and Richard Warren, but unfortunately it stopped abruptly at the point where he was trapped by Cumberland's cordon of troops among the mountains in mid-July. The account, probably abandoned due to bad weather, is now among the Stuart Papers at Windsor, and was published in *A Jacobite Miscellany*, ed. Henrietta Tayler, Roxburghe Club in 1948.

First-hand accounts of many of those involved in the escape were collected by a staunch Jacobite the Reverend Robert Forbes, Bishop of Ross and Caithness, during the years following the rising, and were published under the title *The Lyon in Mourning*, ed. Henry Paton, 3 vols, Scottish History Society, Edinburgh, 1895–6. From Forbes' *Lyon* and other contemporary sources Walter Bigger Blaikie compiled an *Itinerary of Prince Charles Edward Stuart from his Landing in Scotland July 1745 to his Departure in September 1746*, Scottish History Society, 1897.

Those works, supplemented by contemporary and later narratives and biographies, provide a vivid and complete account of the Prince's wanderings.

THE HUNTERS AND THE HUNTED

The following entries detail the major characters in the story of the flight of Bonnie Prince Charlie and relevant key sources. These references do not contain a complete index of *Lyon in Mourning* sources but refer only to principal events during the Prince's escape.

Albemarle, William Anne Keppell, Earl of. Succeeded Cumberland as commander in charge of the search for Prince Charlie. *The Albemarle Papers*, ed. Charles Sanford Terry, Aberdeen, 1902

Burke, Ned. 'Sawnie' MacLeod's servant; guided the Prince from Culloden to the west coast and helped to row him to the Outer Hebrides. After many adventures Burke made his way back to Edinburgh, where he earned his living as a sedan-chair carrier. His account, *Lyon in Mourning*, vol. I, pp. 184, 189–200; I. pp. 163, 166–71, 321–2, 326–9; II, pp. 96, 160

Cameron, Dr Archibald (brother of Lochiel). An important link between the Prince and Lochiel during the flight. Accompanied Charles to France. Executed following the Elibank Plot of 1752. *Lyon*, vol. I, pp. 96, 101, 348–9; II, p. 376; III, pp. 39–42, 45–8, 52, 381–2. Marion F. Hamilton, *The Loch Arkaig Treasure*

Cameron, Revd John, minister at Fort William. His journal. *Lyon*, vol. I, pp. 83–101

Cameron of Clunes, Donald. Lochiel clansman who guided the Prince among mountains. *Lyon*, vol. I, pp. 347–51; III, pp. 39, 45

Cameron of Glen Pean, Donald. Guided Charles safely past enemy cordon on mountains. His own account, *Lyon*, vol. III, pp. 90–4; I, pp. 95, 317–18, 321, 336–41; II, pp. 319, 335–6, 363–4, 376

Cameron of Lochiel, Donald. Wounded at Falkirk and Culloden, but tried to persuade Charles not to flee to France. Sailed with Prince, and died in France two years later. *Lyon*, vol. I, pp. 83–8, 96–101, 174, 348–55; II, pp. 375–80; III, 38–48, 101–3. John Sibbald Gibson, *Lochiel of the '45*, Edinburgh, 1994, brings together information on Lochiel from many sources

Campbell, Donald, of Scalpay. The Prince stayed at his house on the island on the way to Stornoway. *Lyon*, vol. I, pp. 166, 172, 191–2; II, pp. 100–2

Campbell, Major-Gen John, of Mamore. Commander of Argyll militia in search for the Prince. Later became 4th Duke of Argyll. *Lyon*, vol. I, pp. 71, 72, 90, 93, 107, 115, 124, 162, 178–80, 198, 267, 279, 283, 294–7, 303–4, 328, 333, 353, 372–7; II, pp. 32–3, 79, 92, 98–9, 253, 274; III, pp. 123, 127, 189–91. Sir James Fergusson, *Argyll in the Forty-Five*, London, 1951

Cumberland, William Augustus, Duke of. Third son of George II. Culloden was his only victory in an undistinguished military career. Remembered as 'the Butcher' for his cruelty after Culloden. Died 1765. E. Charteris, *William Augustus Duke of Cumberland*, London, 1913. W.A. Speck, *The Butcher. The Duke of Cumberland and the Suppression of the '45*, Oxford, 1981

Elcho, David Wemyss, Lord Elcho. Knew the Prince from boyhood, and followed him all through the '45. Afterwards turned bitterly against Charles. Died in 1787. *Lyon*, vol. I, pp. 160, 190; II, 160; III, 245. *A Short Account of the Affairs of Scotland in the years 1744–6*, Edinburgh, 1907. *Lord Elcho's 'Diary'*, in H. Tayler, *Jacobite Miscellany*, Roxburghe Club, Oxford, 1948

Ferguson, John. Captain of Royal Navy ship *Furnace*. Scoured Hebridean waters in search of Charles' supporters and destroyed much property. Captured Flora MacDonald. *Lyon*, vol. I, pp. 107, 115, 123, 144–5, 160, 180, 193, 198, 297, 303, 305, 312, 328, 372, 374. II, pp. 79, 99, 252–3; III, pp. 22, 84–7, 123, 127, 191. John S. Gibson, *Ships of the Forty-Five*

Glenmoriston men. Eight clansmen who guarded the Prince: Alexander Chisholm, Donald Chisholm, Hugh Chisholm, Patrick Grant, Alexander MacDonald, John MacDonald, Gregor MacGregor and Hugh MacMillan. *Lyon*, vol. II, pp. 365; III, pp. 106–7, 102, 103, 110, 202. Patrick Grant's account, *Lyon*, vol. III, pp. 97–112

Lanzière de Lancize, Chevalier de. French commander. Landed at Loch Broom from the *Bien Trouvé*. Found the Prince in Cameron country. Their secret meeting focused attention on the West Highlands as the place to find an escape ship. John S. Gibson, *Ships of the Forty-Five*. Frank L. McLynn, *France and the Jacobite Rising of 1745*, Edinburgh, 1981

Lockhart of Carnwath, George. *Memoirs Concerning the Affairs of Scotland*, Edinburgh, 1817. Daniel Szechi, *Letters of Lockhart of Carnwath*, Scottish Historical Society, Edinburgh, 1989

Loudoun, James Campbell, Earl of Loudoun. Failed in attempt to ambush the Prince at Moy Hall, and later commanded Argyll militia companies searching for Charles and wreaking vengeance in Highlands. *Lyon*, vol. I, pp. 90–1, 104, 368; II, pp. 34, 35, 78–9, 205; III, pp. 46, 84, 103, 108, 113. Sir James Fergusson, *Argyll in the Forty-Five*, London, 1951

Lovat, Simon Fraser, Lord Lovat. His role in the '45 was discreditable: he did not join, but sent his son to lead Fraser clansmen. He failed to support efforts to continue the rising after Culloden, and was captured and executed in 1747. *Lyon*, vol. I, pp. 68, 190, 321; II, pp. 5, 83–5. W.C. Mackenzie, *Lovat of the Forty-Five*, Edinburgh, 1934

MacDonald, Aeneas. Son of MacDonald of Kinlochmoidart; Paris banker, who largely financed the '45 rising and came to Scotland with Charles and surrendered to General Campbell. Condemned to death, but pardoned, he returned to France where he died in the French Revolution. His account, *Lyon*, vol. I, pp. 281–96; I, pp. 159–60, 201–10, 282–3; III, pp. 50–3

MacDonald, Flora. Escorted the Prince over the sea to Skye dressed as her maid Betty Burke. Later emigrated to Carolina and Nova Scotia. Returned to Skye where she died in 1792. Her account, *Lyon*, vol. I, pp. 296–306; I, pp. 106–24, 130, 196, 302–5, 371–3; II, pp. 13–26, 31–2, 46, 178–80. Letter to Sir John MacPherson, 21 October 1789 in the National Library of Scotland. Hugh Douglas, *Flora MacDonald: The Most Loyal Rebel*, Stroud 1993

MacDonald of Armadale, Hugh. 'Uisdean Cam' ('One-eyed' Hugh). Flora's step-father. Commanded militia hunting the Prince in Hebrides, but secretly helped to arrange escape to Skye. *Lyon*, vol. I, pp. 110, 176, 187–8, 267, 297, 303–4; II, pp. 31–2, 46, 98

MacDonald of Baleshare, Donald Roy. Wounded at Culloden, 'organised' the Skye part of the Flora MacDonald escape plot. *Lyon*, vol. II, pp. 2–35, 42, 46, 72–6, 78, 81, 96–7, 100

MacDonald of Baleshare, Hugh. Involved in Uist part of escape to Skye. His account, *Lyon*, vol. II, pp. 94–103; I, p. 327; II, pp. 7, 29

MacDonald of Barisdale, Coll. Betrayed the Cause and was taken to France as a prisoner. Held in Edinburgh Castle on his return to Scotland, where he died in 1749. *Lyon*, vol. I, pp. 81–2, 88, 91–2, 100

MacDonald of Belfinlay, Ranald. His account, *Lyon*, vol. II, pp. 3–35

MacDonald of Boisdale, Alexander. Half-brother of Clanranald. Begged Charles to abandon rising in 1745, but after Culloden gave much help. Arrested and held at Messenger Dick's house in London along with Flora MacDonald. Freed in 1747. *Lyon*, vol. I, pp. 146–8, 174–7, 205–6, 269, 289, 327; II, pp. 95–8, 256

MacDonald of Borrodale, Aeneas (Angus). Befriended the Prince both at start of the rising and during his time in hiding. Helped Charles to escape to the Outer Hebrides and to hide in the mountains after his return to the mainland. *Lyon*, vol. I, pp. 322–5; II, pp. 252–3; III, p. 377

MacDonald of Borrodale, John. Aeneas (Angus) Borrodale's son. Supplied boat for voyage from Loch nan Uamh to Outer Hebrides, and later guided the Prince among the mountains. His account, *Lyon*, vol. III, pp. 375–83; I, pp. 163, 334

MacDonald of Borrodale, Ranald. Aeneas (Angus) Borrodale's son. With his father, he helped to guide Charles through the mountains. *Lyon*, vol. II, pp. 198, 256, 334

MacDonald of Clanranald. Allan. Catholic priest, known as 'Captain'. Accompanied Charles from Culloden to the Hebrides. Parted with the Prince at Lochboisdale, and arrested with boatman, Donald MacLeod. *Lyon*, vol. I, pp. 163, 167, 321, 323, 325, 326, 330; II, p. 95

MacDonald of Clanranald, Florence. Wife of Clanranald chief, who helped to make Betty Burke costume. *Lyon*, vol. I, pp. 297, 329

MacDonald of Clanranald, Ranald. Clanranald chief. Refused to 'come out' in the rising, but supported the Prince during his flight. *Lyon*, vol. I, pp. 323, 326–7

MacDonald of Clanranald, Ranald (Young Clanranald). Son of chief. Fought for the Prince, and helped him during his flight. *Lyon*, vol. I, pp. 88, 289, 292, 332–5; II, p. 256. *See also* MacDonald of Dalilea

MacDonald of Dalilea, Captain Alexander. Cousin of Flora MacDonald. His account, *Lyon*, vol. III, pp. 84–8. Also account compiled with Young Clanranald and Glenaladale, *Lyon*, vol. I, pp. 321–51

MacDonald of Glenaladale, Alexander. Nephew of Borrodale, wounded at Culloden. Guided the Prince in mountains during flight. Later life was spent in poverty. *Lyon*, vol. I, pp. 90, 95, 97; II, pp. 180, 379; III, pp. 90–1, 97–8, 104, 111, 366–7. *See also* MacDonald of Dalilea

MacDonald of Kingsburgh, Alexander. Factor (land agent) to Sleat chief. Brought Charles to his house when he arrived on Skye with Flora MacDonald. Held for two years in Edinburgh Castle, but never brought to trial. *Lyon*, vol. I, pp. 73–81, 117–22, 126–9, 220; II, pp. 1–3, 13–23, 27, 29, 71–2, 98–102

MacDonald of Kingsburgh, Florence. Wife of Sleat factor. Arrested and questioned about her part in the Prince's stay at Kingsburgh, but freed. *Lyon*, vol. I, pp. xviii, 81, 117–24, 143, 278

MacDonald of Sleat, Sir Alexander. Skye chief; sympathetic to Cause, but government persuaded him not to join the Prince. He raised a militia regiment, which joined in the hunt, but some of his clanspeople, including his wife, helped Charlie's escape. *Lyon*, vol. I, pp. 77–8, 104–7, 161–2, 175, 205–6, 300, 331, 368–72; II, pp. 101–2, 205; III, pp. 108, 113, 187–8. Revd A. and A. MacDonald, *Clan Donald*, 3 vols, Inverness, 1904

MacDonald of Sleat, Lady Margaret. Wife of Sleat chief. Secretly helped Charles with money and presents and was involved in the escape over the sea to Skye. *Lyon*, vol. I, pp. 90, 300; II, p. 8. Revd A. and A. MacDonald, *Clan Donald*, 3 vols, Inverness, 1904

MacDonnell of Glengarry, Alasdair Ruadh. Heir to Glengarry chief. Betrayed Cause by spying for Hanoverians using the name 'Pickle the Spy'. Andrew Lang, *Pickle the Spy*, London, 1897 and *The Companions of Pickle*, London, 1898. Marion F. Hamilton, *The Loch Arkaig Treasure*

MacDonnell of Lochgarry, Donald. In Hanoverian Army, but went over to Charles, becoming a firm supporter. Was with the Prince in Cluny's Cage on Ben Alder, and escaped with him to France. *Lyon*, vol. I, pp. 88, 98, 101, 348–51; III, pp. 39–41, 102–3, 109

MacEachain, Neil. Flora MacDonald's kinsman, who spoke fluent French and Gaelic so was of enormous help to Charles. A quiet, self-effacing man, who played a key part in escape over the sea to Skye. Returned to France where he adopted name MacDonald, and his son later became one of Napoleon's generals. *Lyon*, vol. I, pp. 76–7, 130, 296–301, 330, 373; II, pp. 17n, 20–5; III, p. 22. *Alexis, or the Young Adventurer*, London, 1746. *Narrative*, New Monthly Magazine, 1840. W.B. Blaikie, *Origins of the Forty-Five and Other Papers Relating to the Rising*. Alasdair Maclean, *A Macdonald for the Prince, the Story of Neil MacEachen*, Stornoway, 1982

MacKinnon of Elgol, John. South Skye laird who escorted Charles from Portree, through Cuillins, to Elgol and back to mainland at Mallaig. Captured. His account, *Lyon*, vol. III, pp. 183–8; I, pp. 138, 140–1, 152, 154, 332–3; II, p. 41; III, pp. 183–8, 192–3

MacKinnon of MacKinnon, John. Although a man in his sixties, the clan chief himself escorted the Prince back to mainland from Skye. He was taken prisoner. His account with others including Flora MacDonald, *Lyon*, vol. I, pp. 66–74; I, pp. 141–2, 295, 332–3; II, pp. 81, 98, 253; III, pp.189–90

MacLeod, Alexander ('Sawnie'). The Prince's aide-de-camp; accompanied him after Culloden, and later helped to make contact with officers from French ship *Bien Trouvé*. *Lyon*, vol. I, pp. 88, 98–9, 164, 190, 199, 321; II, p. 160

MacLeod, Donald of Gualtergill. Boatman who sailed with the Prince to Outer Hebrides from Loch nan Uamh and in Outer Isles during May and June. Nicknamed 'Palinurus' after the boatman in the Odyssey. His account, *Lyon*, vol. I, pp. 154–86, 268–9; I, p. 69–70, 194–6, 199–200, 271–4, 322–6; II, pp. 325–6

MacLeod of Brea, Captain Malcolm. Met Charles at Portree, took him to Raasay and back to Skye, he then accompanied him to Elgol where he handed him over to the Mackinnons. His account, *Lyon*, vol. I, pp. 130–42; I, pp. 73–4, 81, 122–3, 174–8, 220, 302; II, pp. 6, 18, 20–31, 48–9, 73–8, 81, 325; III, pp. 48–9, 104–5

MacLeod of Raasay, Malcolm. Chief, who met Charles at Portree and took him briefly to Raasay. *Lyon*, vol. I, p. 145–6; II, pp. 22–6, 79–82; III, p. 123

MacLeod of Raasay, Murdoch. Wounded at Culloden; accompanied Prince to Raasay. His account, *Lyon*, vol. II, pp. 73–8; I, pp. 130–2, 142; II, pp. 6, 20, 26, 29–39, 75–8, 81

MacPherson of Breakachie, Donald. Helped the Prince during latter weeks in hiding, and helped lead him to the escape ships. Stayed behind in Scotland. *Lyon*, vol. II, pp. 375–80; III, pp. 37–48

MacPherson of Cluny, Ewan. Held commission in royal Army, but joined the Prince. At beginning of September 1746 he arranged Charles' last hiding place in hut known as Cluny's Cage on Ben Alder. Remained behind when the Prince sailed. Afterwards he was involved in quarrel over 'Loch Arkaig Treasure'. *Lyon*, vol. I, p. 88; II, pp. 45, 93, 333, 376–8; III, pp. 38–9, 41–8, 121. Marion F. Hamilton, *The Loch Arkaig Treasure*

Murray, Lord George. Charles' able lieutenant-general, but the two quarrelled until Murray resigned leadership. Murray was furious that Charles did not rally his Army at Ruthven after Culloden. Died in Holland in 1760, still loyal to the Cause. *Lyon*, vol. I, pp. 135, 254–67. Winifred Duke, *Lord George Murray and the Forty-Five*, Aberdeen, 1927

Murray of Broughton, John. Charles' Secretary during '45 campaign; too ill to fight at Culloden, but tried to keep campaign alive afterwards. Captured, and turned King's evidence against Lord Lovat. Said to have died in a London madhouse in 1777. *Lyon*, vol. I, pp. 88, 89, 105, 174, 296, 370, II, p. 97, *Memorials of John Murray of Broughton*, ed. R. Fitzroy Bell, Scottish History Society, 1889. *Genuine Memoirs of John Murray of Broughton*, 1747, Edinburgh, 1898

O'Neil, Felix. Arrived from France just before Culloden, and accompanied Charles to the Long Island. Helped to arrange Betty Burke escape, but was left behind when Charles sailed for Skye. Captured and imprisoned. His account, *Lyon*, vol. I, pp. 102–8, 365–79; I, pp. 69, 95, 113, 156–7, 160, 163, 167, 178, 194–6, 296–8, 304, 329–30, 353

O'Sullivan, John William. Irishman in French service, sailed to Scotland with Prince in 1745. Charles accepted his advice over that of Lord George Murray at Culloden. He accompanied the Prince to Long Island, and escaped to France. *Lyon*, vol. I, pp. 69, 102–6, 163, 166–7, 178, 190–1, 194, 268, 298, 321–3, 326, 329–30, 373–4; II, pp. 95–8; III, pp. 11, 375–6. *Journal of the 1745 Campaign and the Wanderings of Prince Charles Edward*, 1746. A. and H. Tayler, *1745 and After*, London, 1938

Scott, Captain Caroline. Violently anti-Jacobite Hanoverian officer; held Fort William when other northern forts fell, ravaged Highlands after Culloden, and scoured Outer Isles for Prince. *Lyon*, vol. I, pp. 71, 93–4, 106–7, 143, 295, 309–10, 335, 370–3; II, pp. 79, 98; III, pp. 16–18, 58, 72

Sheridan, Sir Thomas. Charles' tutor and one of Seven Men of Moidart. Followed the Prince all the way to Derby and back. Escaped, but died in France soon after. *Lyon*, vol. I, pp. 89, 105, 190, 201, 282–4, 370; II, pp. 160, 198. A. and H. Tayler (eds), *Stuart Papers at Windsor*

Stewart, John Roy. Nicknamed 'the Body'. Served in the Prince's Army, and helped in his escape. Returned to France with Charles. *Lyon*, vol. I, pp. 88, 263, 351; II, p. 161; III, pp. 43–4, 382

Walsh, Antoine. Rich merchant and slave trader of Irish descent. Provided ships for the Prince's voyage to Scotland and, after Culloden, played key role in arranging rescue by French ships. Correspondence in Duc de Trémoille, *A Royalist Family, Irish and French and Prince Charles Edward*, Edinburgh, 1904

GENERAL

Manuscript Material

correspondence and reports, Stuart papers at Windsor

government documents, Royal Navy reports and ships' logs, Public Record Office, London

official reports and memoranda, Scottish Record Office, Edinburgh

memoranda relating to French attempts to rescue the Prince, Archives Nationales, Paris

Published Material

Argenson, Marquis d'. *Journal et Mémoires, 1747–8*, ed. E.J.B. Rathery, 9 vols, Paris, 1859–67

Barbier, E.J.F. *Chronique de la Régence et du Règne de Louis XV*, 8 vols, Paris, 1847

Blaikie, W.B. (ed.). *Origins of the Forty-Five and Other Papers Relating to the Rising*, Scottish Historical Society, Edinburgh, 1916

Browne, James. *History of the Highlands and the Highland Clans*, 4 vols, Glasgow, 1832–3

Chambers, Robert. *Jacobite Memoirs of the Rebellion of 1745, 1746, etc.*, Edinburgh, 1827

——. *History of the Rebellion of 1745–6*, Edinburgh, 1869

Doran, John. *'Mann' and Manners at the Court of Florence*, 2 vols, London, 1876

Gibson, John Sibbald. *Ships of the Forty-Five*, London, 1967

Hamilton, Marion F. *The Loch Arkaig Treasure*, Scottish History Society Miscellany, vol. VII, Scottish History Society, Edinburgh, 1941

Home, John. *History of the Rebellion in Scotland*, Edinburgh, 1822

Jarvis, Rupert C. *Collected Papers on the Jacobite Risings*, 2 vols, Manchester, 1971

Johnstone, Chevalier de. *A Memoir of the Forty-Five*, Edinburgh, 1820

Linklater, Eric. *The Prince in the Heather*, London, 1965

Luynes, Duc de. *Mémoires du Duc de Luynes sur la Cour de Louis XV (1735–1758)*, vols IV–VII, Paris, 1861

Maclean, Alasdair and Gibson, John S. *Summer Hunting a Prince*, Stornoway, 1992

Maclean, Sir Fitzroy. *Bonnie Prince Charlie*, London, 1988

McLynn, Frank. *Bonnie Prince Charlie*, London, 1988

Polnay, Peter de. *Death of a Legend*, London, 1952

Selby, John. *Over the Sea to Skye*, London, 1973

Seton, Sir Bruce Gordon and Gordon Arnot, Jean (eds). *The Prisoners of the Forty-Five*, 3 vols, Scottish History Society 3rd series, vols XIII–XV, Edinburgh, 1928–9

Tayler, A. and H. *A Jacobite Exile*, London, 1937

——. *Stuart Papers at Windsor*, London, 1939

Tayler, H. *Jacobite Epilogue*, London, 1941

——. *Two Accounts of the Escape of Prince Charles Edward (with Twelve Letters from Lord George Murray to Andrew Lumisden)*, Oxford, 1951

Tomasson, Katherine. *The Jacobite General*, London, 1958

Ure, John. *A Bird on the Wing*, London, 1992

INDEX

Page references in italic denote illustrations.